CW00664268

THE WOMEN'S
LAND ARMY

Published under the auspices of
THE MINISTRY OF AGRICULTURE AND FISHERIES

THE WOMEN'S LAND ARMY

Vita Sackville-West

UNIFORM

Unicorn Publishing Group
101 Wardour Street
London W1F 0UG

First published 1944

This edition first published by Uniform,
an imprint of Unicorn Publishing Group
© Unicorn Publishing Group, 2016
www.unicornpress.org

A catalogue record for this book is available from
the British Library

ISBN 978-1-910500-18-7

Cover design Unicorn Publishing Group
Typeset by Vivian@Bookscribe

Printed and bound in India by Imprint Digital

Dedicated
by gracious permission
To the Patron of the Women's Land Army
HER MAJESTY THE QUEEN

CONTENTS

APPENDICES

'We could do with thousands more like you..'

JOIN THE
WOMEN'S LAND ARMY

Apply to NEAREST W·L·A COUNTY OFFICE or to W·L·A HEADQUARTERS 6, CHESHAM STREET, LONDON S.W.1

Issued by the Ministry of Labour and National Service in conjunction with the Ministry of Agriculture.

PRINTED FOR H.M. STATIONERY OFFICE BY FOSH & CROSS LTD, LONDON G.313

BAGSHOT PARK

In 1944, when *The Women's Land Army* was published for the first time, Vita Sackville-West was giving an account of an organisation still in the full flow of its service to the country and to the war effort.

During these years, over 240,000 young women joined the Women's Land Army (WLA) and Women's Timber Corps (WTC). Many of these young girls, often from urban dwellings, were only in their teens, living away from home in Britain's most remote and rural landscapes, working up to fifty hours a week in the fields and forests of our country.

This book gives an extraordinary insight into every aspect of the WLA, from the people who ran it to the Land-girls themselves. The voice of the author echoes in your head as you read it, with the tone and diction of the 1940's creating a vivid picture of life as it was for these amazing girls.

At a time when imports of food arrived in this country at the cost of sailors' lives, the dairy goods, meat, vegetables and cereals that the WLA helped to produce saved lives and kept the nation fighting. The contribution the Land-girls made to our country must never be underestimated nor forgotten, whether they were growing produce, keeping livestock, controlling rats, managing trees and hedges, or helping organise and run this incredibly diverse and widespread civilian army, we must remind ourselves that they had volunteered to join and make a difference to the war effort.

In 2014 I was extremely honoured to unveil a memorial to the WLA and the WTC and to meet a number of those who had served. Most of the stories they shared with me that day were of happy times alongside the hard work and long hours, but some were of hardship and endurance and misery. Whatever their individual experiences I hope they feel their significant contribution has now been suitably remembered.

I also hope the younger generations who read *The Women's Land Army* will see it as a fine tribute to the achievements of their mothers, grandmothers and great grandmothers.

HRH The Countess of Wessex GCVO

I

Introductory

We have grown tired of hearing the Land Army described as the Cinderella of the women's services; it has a sort of self-pitying sound. But this, in many ways, it really is. Not for the Land Army are the community existence, the parades, the marchings-past, the smart drill, the eyes-right, the salutes – or very seldom. For the most part its members work isolated and in a mouse-like obscurity. Their very uniform seems to suggest a bashful camouflage of green-and-fawn to be lost against the grass or the stubble. It is seldom that the Land-girl emerges into the streets of great cities; when she appears in public at all, it is in the village or the little country town, for by the very nature of her occupation she is rural, not urban. Yet often in her previous occupation she has been urban enough. She has been a shop-assistant, a manicurist, a hairdresser, a shorthand-typist, a ballet dancer, a milliner, a mannequin, a saleswoman, an insurance clerk. She has worn silk stockings and high-heeled shoes, pretty frocks and jaunty hats; has had plenty of fun, being young and gay; has done her job during the working hours, and then at the end of the day has returned to her personal life among friends or family, entertainment or home. At a moment's notice she has now exchanged all that; instead of her silks and georgettes she wears wool and corduroy and clumping boots; her working-hours seem never definitely to end, for on the land there may always be a sudden urgent call; she lives among strangers, and the jolly atmosphere of homely love or outside fun is replaced often by loneliness and boredom. She gets up at an hour when other people are still warmly asleep and although dawn in spring or summer may be a moment one should be sorry to miss, a dingy wet morning in the winter before the light has even begun to clear the eastern sky is a very different story; she goes to bed with aching muscles after a dull evening, knowing that next morning the horrible alarm will shrill through her sleep, calling her back to her damp boots, her reeking oilskin, and the mud and numbing cold outside. All this she has done, and is doing, so that *we* may eat. Nor has she always done it under the threat of a compulsory calling-up, but often voluntarily before her age-group was reached.

'Why did you chuck your good job before you need?'

'I just couldn't bear to see other girls in all sorts of uniform and feel I was doing nothing but sell shoes in a lovely shop.'

Whenever one is dealing with human beings in the mass, some very odd and unforeseen factors emerge. They are most revealing, and demonstrate how much at fault one was in any pre-conceived estimate of how people were likely to react in given circumstances. Thus it was astonishing to find that one-third of the Land Army volunteers came from London or our large industrial cities; and astonishing to note the tragic disappointment shown by those who could not be accepted for country work because they were more urgently needed elsewhere. This surprising fact does suggest that there are many townspeople who feel they would prefer the country, in complete contradiction to the popular view that the youth of today is wedded to the cities.

II

The Formation of the WLA

Of course it would be absurd to pretend that everything in the Land Army had invariably been perfect, and that the conduct of every girl had been model, heroic, and in every way beyond reproach. Such a contention would carry no conviction and would tend only to diminish any further record of the very real merit of the majority. The Land Army is composed of human beings, not machines, like any other service or corporate collection of people; and it is in the nature of human beings to be both various and fallible. Since we all know that, it is better and more convincing to admit straight away that some girls can be unbearably tiresome; some downright ill-behaved; that some have proved unable or unwilling to stand the work; that some farmers have been recalcitrant; some officials lacking in understanding; some landladies unreasonable; some wives jealous; some mackintoshes leaky; some boots too tight. But, taken all in all, the girls themselves have been amazingly good, plucky, and competent; the most prejudiced farmers have largely come round; and the uniform outfit has been greatly improved as the years went by. After this preamble and generalisation, we may come down to the brass tacks of how the WLA was formed, how it is organised, what its functions and achievements are, the Land-girl herself, her problems, her welfare, and her future; but in order not to overload the text with too many figures, a number of tables have been placed separately at the end.

III

Headquarters at Balcombe

During the war of 1914–18, which we used, so mistakenly, to call the Great War, a Women's Land Army was not called into existence until the war had been going on for three years. It was not until 1917, when there was only about three weeks' food supply in the whole country, that the Minister of Agriculture, Mr Rowland Prothero (who later became Lord Ernle) determined to create this new organisation under the directorship of Dame Meriel Talbot. This is not the place to give an account of what was then accomplished, but for purposes of comparison, every thing now being on a far vaster scale, we may note the difference in the enrolment figures – 23,000 the maximum number by 1918, and over 80,000 by 1943. The difference in the time of formation is also remarkable, for, far from waiting three years, the present WLA sprang into being even before war had been declared. Undeceived by the promises of Munich, a most praiseworthy foresight had been shown. On June 1st, 1939, in fact, the organisation was formed, with the result that by September, when the call came, a thousand volunteers could immediately be sent into employment, many of them already trained. There is a story of one eager volunteer who begged to be allowed to join the WLA as she 'felt she must be something to impede the war effort,' and of another who had put her name down and was rung up on September 1st, 1939, and told to hold herself in readiness. 'How long can you give me?' she asked; 'twenty minutes?'

Four months later, by the end of December, Land-girls in employment already totalled 4,544.*

The WLA is a part of the Ministry of Agriculture and Fisheries, and can have had no kinder or more co-operative friend than the Minister of Agriculture, Mr Robert Hudson, but (as in the last war) it is entirely staffed and run by women. The Hon. Director from the first has been Lady Denman, DBE, who is not only, by common consent, the most competent and experienced of chairmen, but who has with extreme generosity given over her own home, Balcombe Place (see page 17), as the general head-quarters. Imagine a baronial hall thus transformed. The red velvet curtains still hang heavily in their place, the oak panelling still makes a rich and sombre background, but the splendid rooms are now filled with office-desks and trestle tables, piled with card-indexes and stationery, typewriters and telephones, pots of paste and Stickphast. Green and white posters of Land-girls leading horses, Land-girls carrying corn-sheaves, are tacked up with drawing-pins against the walls. Busy young women

---

*See Appendix I, employment figures, on page 172

carrying folders run nimbly up and down the wide oak staircase; the doors of the rooms on the upper floor, which once were spare bedrooms, are now labelled with the designation of the office department to be found within. In one window embrasure sits the editorial staff of *The Land-girl* monthly magazine with a circulation of over 21,000 copies, under the direction of Mrs Pyke, whose editorial note on the cover is surely a model of what such notes should be. Nor is the activity of this hive restricted to the house itself. Out of doors, in the garden and on the now sacrificed lawn-tennis courts, is a variety of livestock personally tended by different members of the staff:

geese, rabbits, poultry, pigs, so that in the morning before breakfast you may meet a Regional Officer returning with her empty pails, in a dripping mackintosh but with glowing cheeks, and one wonders whether after this little bit of personal experience she does not sit down to her desk with an increased sympathy for the girls whose daily round is composed of just such things.

One of the queerest sights in the transformation of Balcombe, is the occupation by Land Army uniform of the outbuildings the garages, the stables, and the squash-rackets court. These evidences of luxury have become purely utilitarian; they have been turned into warehouses. There, from floor to ceiling, are stacked the familiar green jerseys, the brown breeches, the black gum-boots, the fawn overcoats, the pale Aertex shirts. All so neat, so beautifully piled. It gives one some idea of the work involved in supplying the needs of eighty thousand girls. One is accustomed to seeing one Land-girl at a time, or perhaps a little bunch of them in a gang, but here one gets some impression of the horde which, in the aggregate, the girls who 'fight in the fields' really represent.*

---

* HQ have now, May 1944, been transferred to 6, Chesham Street, SW1.

IV

Organisation at Headquarters

Lady Denman, who has thus patriotically given over the whole of her home and the whole of her time to the national cause (she is also Chairman of the Federation of Women's Institutes), is. supported in her administrative work by Mrs Jenkins, CBE, the Assistant Director, and by a cohort of able women to whom the running of special branches is delegated.

Apart from the immediate seconds and thirds in command, there are seven Regional Officers, each of whom is in charge of one or several counties. They are really liaison officers between headquarters and the counties, and their job is the double one of (*a*) seeing that the counties understand and carry out the policy indicated to them in circular letters, smoothing over any difficulties which may arise, and (*b*) bringing back to headquarters for solution any particular local or regional problem. All these Regional Officers pay regular visits to the counties in their charge and maintain a close and constant contact with the officials in each county.

So much for the means of keeping touch between the big, pumping heart at the centre and the ends of the arteries which reach out to every county office in England and Wales, but in addition to this some idea of the intricate work carried on at headquarters should be gained from a short and abridged list of the general routine administration, plus questions of policy concerning wage-rates, recruitment, conditions of employment, and so on. Everybody today knows how laborious is any negotiation where any Government department is concerned; not because the Government department wishes to be unnecessarily obstructive; on the contrary, it would probably welcome any reduction of its clerical labours; but because of the enormous complication involved in running a population of millions in times of war. Have we not all raged against the forms we have to fill up to obtain what would seem to be the simplest concession? We tend to forget that we are not just one isolated individual, wanting one modest thing, but a unit amongst multiplied crowds all wanting the same, or another, modest thing. The knots in the network woven for the best possible good of the greatest number, are necessarily myriad; and it is as well that we the uninitiated, who sometimes incline to become impatient, should from time to time be startled into an understanding of how such matters work. Thus, it must be remembered that in the last resort the Treasury is responsible for the expenditure of public money; and that the Treasury is almost morbidly conscientious in such respects. This leads to a lot of delay; but what tax-payer, when he comes to think of it, will quarrel with that? This is merely an example of the quite reasonable reason which

Gertrude Mary Denman, Baroness Denman, DBE

usually can be found to underlie most restrictions, if once you get to the bottom of it.

How often have I heard a Land-girl exclaim, 'Why can't they give us another type of (*a*) shirt, (*b*) boots, (*c*) mac? Why do we have to be mobile? Why can't they arrange for us to work near our homes? Why can't I work on the farm where my friend is working? Why do they take my coupons from me?' and so on endlessly. There is always this vague 'they' in the background; mean, voracious, obdurate, disobliging. 'They' seem to think it impossible ever to make an exception to a rule. Surely 'they' must see that my case is quite different from anybody else's case?

One tries to explain that things are not quite so simple as all that.

Thus, the Women's Land Army has of course primarily to deal with its own Ministry, of Agriculture, but this is not the end of the matter, for many other Government departments and various bodies may also be concerned. Recruiting, for instance, depends upon agreement with the Ministry of Labour, and ultimately with the War Cabinet. Questions affecting wages are subject to discussion with the Agricultural Wages Board, the National Farmers' Union, the National Union of Agricultural Workers, and the Transport and General Workers' Union, and must also be frequently discussed with the Ministry of Labour. The requisitioning and equipment of Land Army hostels depend upon the co-operation of the Ministry of Supply, the Ministry of Labour, and the Ministry of Works. Office accommodation and equipment have to be negotiated with the Ministry of Works and the Stationery Office. As for uniform, it is not sufficient to place an order (which anyhow must be done six or eight months in advance to meet all possible needs), with the Ministry of Supply, but the Materials Committee of that Ministry may also have to be consulted, in conjunction with the Board of Trade and numerous controls of which the Land-girl, naturally, has never heard, such as the Rubber Control, the Leather Control, the Cotton Control... The Ministry of Fuel and Power has a say in the allocation of all petrol allowances. The Press and publicity must not be forgotten, and this task falls to one specially appointed officer at headquarters. Records must also be kept, and for this purpose a master-index is piled against the panelled walls of Balcombe, containing a register of every volunteer of the many thousands who have passed through the Land Army's hands. Welfare demands a separate section with the appropriate staff; and, finally, annual estimates must be prepared for submission to the Treasury. These, of course, are extremely detailed, and must include all estimated expenditure for the coming financial year: the expenses of the fifty-two County Offices, staff salaries, travelling, postage, costs of training, hostels, and all uniform supplies likely to be required.

From time to time conferences are held in London, where 'the counties' meet Lady Denman and the leading officials of her staff and may freely express their views on any question of policy or of detail. Information is given out, concerning change or revision in the regulations, intricate legal points are reduced to elementary simplicity by the Assistant Director, and then Lady Denman as chairman, leaning back with a cigarette, invites comment. I don't know how it affects these ladies from all over the kingdom, but I do know that it made me feel very English indeed, when one after the other stood up and announced herself not by her own name but by the name of the county she represented – 'Norfolk! Devon! Warwick!' – all come together with the same purpose in the service of their country. It reminded me of the map one used to have in the schoolroom, showing one's little triangular island cut up into jig-saw patches of different colours, only here the patches were suddenly personified, dressed in honest tweeds and rather strong shoes. I felt how much, how very much, I liked the English; how much, how very much, how painfully much, I loved England.

V

Organisation in the Counties

Next in order to the controlling staff at headquarters come the County Offices. Every county has its Organising Secretary, its office staff, its Chairman, its Committee, its sub-committees, and its Local Representatives, known in some counties as Village Registrars. In the case of the larger counties, or counties with a very high figure of employment, they may be divided into East and West, each with a separate office, as in Kent, Suffolk and Sussex. The three Ridings in Yorkshire and the three divisions in Lincolnshire, each have their separate offices. In some cases two or more counties combine: Leicestershire with Rutland, Cumberland with Westmorland, Cambridgeshire with Huntingdon; and in Wales, Anglesey with Carnarvon, Merioneth, and Montgomery; Brecon with Radnor; Cardigan with Carmarthen and Pembroke.

The salaried workers are the County Secretaries and the staff employed in the County Offices; also the county organisers who are the field workers of the county office; but the Chairman, the Committee members, and the Representatives are all voluntary and unpaid.

In considering the work at headquarters we were concerned with the larger questions of policy and general administration, but coming down in the scale we get to the detail. We come closer to the Land-girl herself; we enter the region where she becomes an individual. At headquarters she was a number, one of many thousands, neatly filed for reference in that master index; her uniform waited cold, uncrumpled, with no darns, no patches, in the high heaps safely warehoused; but now in the counties she has a personality, a name, a nickname even; her jersey is warmed by her young body, her dungarees have lost their creases, they have got stains on the knees; she has her small possessions put out in her billet, the photographs, perhaps an ornament or two; she has her worries, and her Representative to whom she can tell them. She is no longer WLA No. 657085, she is Betty or Madge or Nan, or (as one girl I met was charmingly called) Winsome.

The County Offices are of course in close personal touch with the girls in their own county. A girl *may* be placed in employment in the county she belongs to, but often she goes far from home in order to satisfy a demand for labour in some other county whose local supply has run short. One essential condition imposed on a volunteer for the Land Army is that she must be mobile and must go without protest wherever she is sent. About one-third of the recruits come from London and Middlesex, or from industrial towns in Lancashire and Yorkshire; so, taken all in all, the girl who works in her own county is one of a lucky minority. Again, a number of girls have been brought principally from the North to compose threshing-gangs in counties with a large arable acreage. Again, many English girls have found their way into Wales. Some have come from the Dominions, and although the WLA may not have attracted so many overseas volunteers as the other Services, those who have come on to the English land from other parts of the Empire have notoriously turned their experience of agriculture in their own countries to very good account here.

The County Offices have their methods for collecting a good deal of data about the volunteer. In practically every county, proper interviewing sessions are held. Interviewers are carefully chosen people; they may be Committee members or others; and the sessions are usually attended by the County Organiser. It is a regulation that every volunteer must be interviewed by not less than two people.

In the big cities interviewing is nearly a whole-time job. Volunteers may now (1944) apply for enrolment only by permission of the Employment Exchanges, but the responsibility for organising the interviewing sessions still rests with the WLA County Office.

In some rural areas, however, the enrolment of the volunteer may start off with an interview conducted by the Representative nearest to the girl's home address. This interview is meant to be friendly rather than formal, and much will depend upon the interviewer's perception and tact. She must make every allowance for the girl being reserved and shy, especially when, as often happens, an anxious and somewhat suspicious mother is hovering round, eager to put in a word, or far too many words. She has to ascertain certain facts – the girl's full name, age, present occupation, whether she can ride a bicycle, whether she possesses one, whether she had had any experience of country life and if so what? All these, and some others of the same nature, are set questions; but privately the interviewer is of course sizing up the girl and forming her own estimate of her intelligence, physique, and general suitability. Should she decide that the volunteer can probably be accepted, she will get her to sign a form of undertaking, by which she accepts registration as a member of the WLA and promises to hold herself available for service on the land wherever she may be needed, also that should circumstances arise which prevent her from carrying out this promise she will ask her County Secretary for permission to resign and will return the uniform and badge with which she has been supplied.

All is not over yet, for she must first obtain a medical certificate from an approved doctor, the fee being paid for her by the Ministry of Agriculture; and, as may be imagined, a strong and healthy physique is essential for the work she is seeking to undertake. But supposing she successfully passes all these preliminary enquiries, she is then passed on to the County Office, when in due course she becomes a full-blown member of the WLA, and will finally be posted either to a farm or to a training centre. Here, for the moment, we will leave her, for there still remains something to say about the work of the various county officials.

VI

The Work of the Representatives

The County Office is careful to establish a personal relationship with the girls, but in an even more constant and immediate contact are the District Representatives. The task of the 'Rep' is not always enviable. It is extremely personal and thus calls for the exercise of considerable tact and sympathy. But as we have been candid about the girl, even to the point of calling her unbearably tiresome at times, and at times downright ill-behaved, let us be equally candid about the Rep and her own short-comings. Let us recognise that she usually belongs to a different class of birth and upbringing, and also (which is quite as significant) to a different generation. It is terribly difficult to adjust or even to modify an outlook which has grown up with you for half a century; terribly difficult to be tolerant and understanding of a code which may consistently outrage your own. It is perhaps a little unfair to set every well-meaning Rep down as 'Lady Blimp,' but let us at least recognise that some divergence of point of view must inevitably arise between the staid squirearchy of middle-age, and gay wild youth out for all the fun it can get.

The Rep has to adjust herself as best she can to this and to other problems. First there is the girl, with her difficulties, her grievances, her requests, sometimes her serious troubles, sometimes, alas, her reprehensible behaviour. With all these, and Heaven knows they can be varied, the Rep has to deal. The innumerable troubles incident on human life all naturally seem to muster in the Land-girl's repertoire: health, love, morals, finance, disputes, resentments, restlessness... The Land-girl does not work in a corporate body; she cannot be moved about in numbers as a Service unit can be moved about; she cannot really be ordered about at all, she can only be persuaded. The Rep has no appeal except to the girl's own willingness and good sense. No disciplinary measures can be taken, either for absenteeism, slackness, unpunctuality, or bad work. She can, it is true, be dismissed altogether, but this is an excessive measure which the WLA is unwilling to take except in cases of extreme provocation. Wastage is a serious consideration, and the disappearance of a trained or partially trained girl is a loss to agriculture to be avoided wherever possible.

There are some perfectly good reasons for this absence of discipline, though sometimes the harassed Rep may feel that the power of a threatening hint would not come amiss in her armoury. Briefly, here are the reasons advanced to counter the criticisms which have sometimes been made. Why, people ask, should the WLA not be organised and run on the same basis as the three Women's Auxiliary Services? These people perhaps overlook the fact that the three Women's Auxiliary Services, the ATS, the WAAF, the

WRNS, are in truth ancillary to the three Fighting Services, and that is why they must be formed and must work on strictly military lines. They are, moreover, employed by the State; whereas the enormous majority of Land-girls are employed by individual farmers. You cannot order a girl three days detention in a farmhouse or in her billet. The whole thing is on a completely different basis, the difference between the military and the civil, and those who are so ready with their criticism would do well to remember that the same condition applies to all workers in civil industries, however vital their production. No one ever seems to suggest that workers in factories or mines or dockyards should be subject to military law. The name Women's Land Army may perhaps be responsible for this confusion in the public mind, though no one imagines that the Land-girl carries a revolver in her breeches' pocket.

The Rep, then, has no hold over a recalcitrant volunteer, save such influence as she may be able personally to exert. True, she can threaten dismissal, but the girl who has brought her to this point probably does not care; in fact, she may actually be anxious to get out of the WLA in order to enter some other occupation which she thinks more attractive. It is all quite inevitable, but it does not make the task of the Rep any easier. Even the form of undertaking which the volunteer has signed upon enrolment, promising to give her services for the duration of the war, is not legally binding. The Rep, however, if she sees that it is hopeless to try and smooth matters over, will report to the County Office, who will then usually prefer to let a girl go rather than retain a reluctant worker. In this case, she is reported to the Ministry of Labour and transferred into some other kind of national service.

Some curious reasons for resignation are sometimes given. One girl said she didn't feel she was being very useful in the WLA, but felt sure she would be doing some good on the ENSA programme.

It happens also that the Rep has to deal with either a disgruntled or a downright unreasonable farmer – the exception, I should hasten to add. Here, on the face of it, it would seem an admirable system to appoint local representatives who are already acquainted with the farmers in their district, but sometimes it works out very awkwardly. It is much more difficult to go and make yourself disagreeable to a neighbour with whom you are on friendly terms, than to descend anonymously in an angry official capacity and say harsh firm things about wages and overtime. Still, she has a backing here, for she can always get the County Office to write the letter saying that his Land-girl will be taken away if matters do not mend; taken away *and not replaced*. However much a farmer may grumble, there are few, when it comes to the point, who want that to happen.

Then there is the question of billeting. That is nominally the responsibility of the employer, but very often it becomes the poor Rep's responsibility too. She gets a letter saying that Mr Truelove of Honeysuckle Farm requires three girls urgently, can't find anywhere to put them, and will she please do something about finding accommodation. She sighs. She has no compulsory powers, and she knows that every housewife within miles has either let her spare room already, or for some reason is unwilling to have a guest in her house. 'These Land-girls, with their dirty boots, and wanting their lunch packed up for them and a hot meal in the evening – no thank you.'

Truly, the Rep's is not always an enviable job. But it has its compensations. It takes her into the farms and the stack-yards; it takes her over the fields; it brings her into a new kind of contact with many pleasant and homely, people; it takes her into many a genial kitchen at supper-time, when the white tablecloth is spread under the lamp and the table is set with yellow plates, and there is a huge loaf and a bowl of tomatoes and jade-green lettuce in the centre. The fire glows behind the bars of the grate, the kettle bubbles gently. The man of the house sits in his shirt-sleeves reading the newspaper while he waits for his tea, the children stare, the dog gets up, the housewife comes out from the scullery wiping her hands, and there is the Land-girl in the midst of them, young, pretty, healthy, almost like the daughter of the family.

It is in moments like these that the Rep can feel her work rewarded; when she sees the smile of real welcoming pleasure; when she gains the shy confidence and feels that she is regarded as a friend, not as a dragon; when the snapshot of the young man is produced to show her; even when there is the release of tears and the reliance upon her sympathy. Headquarters, more severely official, discourages the possessive 'my girls' which every Rep uses; but really, you can scarcely blame her. She has earned the right.

I should not, however, like to give the impression that the well-being of the Land-girl is vested entirely in the hands of the local well-wisher, Lady Bountiful, Lady Blimp, or whatever she may be. Something far more ponderous and tabulated lies behind the pretty watercolour that I have sketched. The whole responsible organisation of the County Office lies behind it – I had almost written 'machinery' instead of organisation, but machinery seems too dour a word. Organisation, then; and what does that mean? It means, in effect, that the Rep is nothing more than the link between the girl and the County Office which eventually has to deal with any real problem reported. The Rep acts only as the eyes and ears of the County Office; she is the liaison officer, no more. In the end, it is the County Secretary who must see that all conditions of employment, such as wages, overtime-pay and sick-pay, holidays and days off, are properly adhered to. And if the Rep isn't doing her job properly, it is up to the County Secretary to send the County Organiser to look into the matter. Nothing is left to mere goodwill, or to chance.

Thus, the Rep has definite instructions. She is supposed

to visit every Land-girl in her district once a month, and the Table on p. 176 will give some idea of the detailed information she is supposed to collect. As may be imagined, it is no sinecure for the Rep who has to track down both the Land-girl and her employer both out on their various tasks, and God knows where to be found on outlying acres of the farm. The information thus painfully and muddily acquired, however, supplies the real safeguard for the volunteer.

Nor does the work of the good Rep end there. It is her business also to introduce the newcomer to her country neighbours; to the Women's Institute; to the Young Farmers' Club; and to tell her all about the Land Army activities arranged for her benefit, the correspondence courses, the proficiency tests, and the clubs which numbered nearly six hundred by January, 1944.

There is certainly a lot to be said for the good Rep and certainly a lot for her to do, in her humble position of link between the girl on the job and the People at the Top.

VII
The Land-girl

Having thus worked our way through the rind and the shell of the nut, we reach the kernel, which is the Land-girl herself. She is the important thing in the whole story. Except in the (fortunately rare) instances where she has been called on to meet danger and emergency, her story is not sensational. It is a plodding story, of endurance rather than heroics, and she should be richly honoured for having chosen her vital and exacting role so thoroughly away from the limelight. In this war-drama with its innumerable cast and its gigantic stage, she has seldom had the chance to strut within view of the audience. Rallies and processions have occasionally given her the chance, but in her daily life the arc-lights have not streamed down upon her green and brown. She has remained always behind the wings. When she took up her job she knew quite well that this would be the case, she knew quite well that she wasn't going to be showy.

Perhaps she didn't always know how hard the life was going to be. Perhaps she had visions of herself teaching gentle little calves to suck her finger in a bucket of milk She came, remember, in many instances from a very different kind of life, scarcely knowing, as country people say, 'one end of a cow from the other.' It was all very well for the country-born girls, who did at least know what they were going into; girls who had probably done some seasonal work on farms during their holidays, even if they were not actually the daughters of farmers. Many of these had gone away into a more urban employment, but when they returned to the land they were going back into something not totally unfamiliar. Their hands might have got softened in shop or office life, their muscles weakened, and their standard of comfort raised; but at least they knew what they were letting themselves in for. The town-bred girl didn't always know. Her idea of the country was a summer-holiday idea, when you strolled down a Hampshire lane picking wild flowers to which you couldn't put a name, or lay in the sun on the Sussex Downs sniffing the thyme and the gorse, and thinking that although it was all very peaceful and restful for a week you couldn't really stand this sort of thing for ever. How did some people stand it? You supposed they did or there woudn't be anybody living in the country at all.

And even so, in seeing this, just the wild-flowers and the gorse and the larks, the prettiness and peace and restfulness of the country, and thinking how agreeable it was as a change for a week, but slow! so slow you couldn't stand it for long, she was seeing only one side of country life. She might admire a great golden slope of corn, but never thought – why should she? – of the long and complicated process which had gone to produce it, nor of the labour which would be expended on it before it turned into a loaf on her own breakfast table. Still less did she ever think that she herself might become involved in all those fatiguing mysteries....

Yet here she is. She is in the bumping seat of the tractor, looking carefully over her shoulder to make sure she is getting the furrow straight. She is cold, and the rain drives in her face, for there is no protection on a tractor against the weather. Now she is stooking, and this time she is hot; too hot; so hot that she wonders how long she can go on; for it is full summer and there is no shade out in the harvest field. She is pitching the heavy sheaves up on the cart. She is in the stack-yard, the threshing machine grinding and clanking; her head is tied up in a scarf, she wears a cellophane shield over her eyes, the grit and chaff fly all around her, up her nose, down her throat; she is dirty as a sweep; the machine-proprietor swears at her...Or she is out in the snowy forest, her fingers numbed with handling the slippery frosty logs. Or she is up to her ankles in water, clearing a ditch. Nobody sees her; nobody but the men whose ordinary life it has always been, and who, she knows, will be only too glad of a chance to catch her out.

A gloomy picture? It might seem so, but the outstanding thing about the Land-girl is that she isn't gloomy at all. On the contrary, anyone who has seen her about, in her few hours off duty, must concede that she looks the most cheerful of mortals. It is always possible to paint any picture in dark colours, but that means that one has left out the essential part, which is the illumination of the spirit playing over it. Life depends largely on how you take it, and there can be no question that the vast majority of these girls, with their youth, their resilience, and their health to carry them through, take it in the gayest possible spirit. You have only to look at them, anywhere; and, after all, 80,000 young women cannot all be pretending a cheerfulness they do not feel.

And yet, in the streets you do not see them at their best. They are dressed-up then, for their outing, and there is surely no one who can do more extraordinary things with a uniform than the Land-girl who has really put her mind to it. It is such a pity, because the Land Army uniform, well-worn, can be as becoming as any uniform now walking about the country. It is a source of despair to the poor Land Army official, who knows better than anybody how well these girls deserve to be taken seriously, and who is compelled to watch *some* of them exposing themselves to a thoughtless ridicule. I know how much I minded when a smart young officer in the ATS asked me: 'Why on earth do you people let some of your girls go about making such guys of themselves? If one of our girls were seen dressed half in uniform and half in civvies, with her hat nearly falling off the back of her head, she would very soon get ticked off.'

Guys... It wasn't an agreeable word, and the answer, when I gave it, didn't sound very convincing. But it was an answer which must be repeated here, because it meets comprehensively many of the criticisms aimed from time to time at the unfortunate Land Army. It was the same statement that we have already recorded in dealing with the difficulties of the Rep, namely, that members of the Land Army are *not* subject to military discipline. The Land-girl can't be controlled in matters relating to her personal life; and, being young and feminine, she regards her clothes as very personal indeed. The young, whether masculine or feminine, are healthily, though not always rightly, convinced that they know best, and any elderly person throwing out a hint, however tactful, is immediately set down as an old stuffy. I suppose that this is as it should be; but I have sometimes wondered what the girl of this war would say to some of the regulations which applied to her predecessor in the last war: she mustn't be seen smoking in public, she mustn't put her hands in her pockets, and she mustn't be seen without an overall after working hours... Presumably breeches were things to be covered up as soon as possible. I have sometimes thought also that if this minority (luckily it is only a minority) could hear the remarks passed upon them behind their backs, even by their own contemporaries, they might pause to consider that uniform properly worn is smart, whereas uniform adapted to the personal whimsy of the wearer looks like nothing but a confused and unsuccessful fancy-dress. However, it is no good telling them. It is no good even pointing out that they would think it comical in the extreme if they encountered a soldier wearing a battle dress tunic on the upper part of his body, grey flannel trousers on his legs, and a Trilby hat coquettishly perched on one side of his head. Yet they themselves will cheerfully go about in a flowery frock showing under their khaki overcoat, or a magenta jumper combined with dungarees. And as for the things some of them do with their hats and their hair! ...

The Land-girl is given a brown felt slouch hat, intended to be worn straight over reasonably controlled hair. She could look as romantic as a cowboy in it if she liked; and indeed, on a reduced scale, it is not unlike the hats affected by the once popular Tom Mix and his colleagues. The trouble is that she forgets all about the Tom and remembers only the Mix. She mixes her own desire to look fashionable with the original intention of the Ministry of Agriculture, which was to provide her with a hat designed for the work she had to do, supplying a shady brim over the eyes and a protection for the back of her neck. The result is neither one thing nor the other. It is neither useful, romantic, nor smart in either the uniform or the fashionable sense. It is merely comic, as comic as a music-hall turn.

You cannot look fashionable in uniform; you can usually look only trim, neat and correct; but the Land-girl's uniform does offer the other alternative of looking picturesque. This alternative she too often neglects in favour of trying to imitate the millinery advertisements in the illustrated papers. With dire results. She builds her hair up in such a way that no hat could possibly be expected to remain in place, adds a bootlace to her hat, and uses it as a chin-strap, trying, presumably, to make an ornament out of it, not realising that to the casual observer she looks as though she were suffering either from toothache or from mumps. One wonders if she has ever looked at herself in the mirror...

As a matter of fact, she seldom wears her hat at all when working. She keeps it for her hours off duty, which is when the public see it and have this opportunity to scoff. When working, if she doesn't prefer to go bareheaded, she usually ties her head up in a coloured scarf, a practice which I find pretty, practical, peasant-like, and consequently pleasing. It seems to me suitable, somehow, that our Land-girls should instinctively have adopted this tradition from the agricultural women workers of other lands. It puts me in mind of women turning the hay in Alpine meadows, and of women harvesting the huge orange pumpkins on farm lands in France.

But all this is by far too superficial a criticism of the Land-girl. It would be a pity to dwell on it for too long. One just wishes, for her own sake, that she wouldn't. It does not affect her real merit in the least. It amounts to saying no more than that she is young, vain, obstinate, and in some ways mistaken and rather silly. One is sorry, only, that she should sometimes expose herself to sarcastic remarks about 'making a guy of herself,' when in fact she is such a solid and enduring person.

For she has much to endure.

Anybody who has any experience of a land-worker's life will realise this, even those who have been brought up to it with its roughs and its smooths, its good weather and its bad.

Instead of criticising her small vagaries, let us consider what she does, remembering always that in the majority of cases she isn't a country-bred girl at all, but a relatively spoilt and gently nurtured girl from the town and even the city. The best way to appreciate what she does will be to give a list of her various occupations, and then to peer for more detail into a close-up of what those occupations involve.

She milks; she does general farm-work which includes ploughing, weeding, hoeing, dung-spreading, lifting and clamping potatoes and other root crops, brishing and laying hedges, cleaning ditches, haymaking, harvesting, threshing; in more specialised ways, she prunes and sprays fruit-trees, picks and packs the fruit, makes and lays thatch, makes silage, pulls flax, destroys rats, works an excavator, reclaims bad land, works in commercial gardens and private gardens, works in the forests felling timber, measuring timber, planting young trees... It is quite an impressive list; and I think everyone will agree that it argues a high degree of adaptability on the part of British young womanhood.

Now let us take a closer look.

VIII
Milking

 She milks. I put this first for several reasons. Partly because it is one of the most important jobs that the WLA has undertaken; partly because it is also one of the most exacting; partly because it is one at which the Land-girl has excelled.

It is one of the most important because, as everybody now knows, milk-production is a vital part of our agricultural industry. Young children have to be supplied with milk, in new and extra quantities to supplement the nourishment they might otherwise lack; and then there is the normal supply to private houses and cottages in rural districts; and also the bulk supply of milk in churns to the distributing co-operative centres. All this means very early hours for the milker. It means getting up at half-past five or even five in the morning, in the dark for half of the year, in the wet and the cold and the slush; and all this, so that the churns may go off on the lorry in time and the sealed bottle may stand duly delivered for breakfast on everybody's doorstep. These things happen as though by magic to the ordinary citizen; he seldom thinks, and why should he? of what it has meant to the unseen unknown somebody somewhere.

Somebody in the dark country, splashing her way down a muddy lane with the little yellow spotlight circle of her torch on the ground to guide her. She may not be 'feeling too good' that morning, but still she has to go. She is young, tender; and the bed she has left was very warm. She exchanges this, very often, for a long walk or bicycle-ride in the morning black-out between her billet and the farm. Sometimes she is even frightened: town-people are notoriously alarmed by the silence and emptiness of the country, and the country before anyone else is astir can be very silent and empty indeed. She is quite alone. The hedges on either side of the

lane are lined with sinister shapes. A twig cracks, and she nearly screams. But the people in England, and the children of England, must have their milk. She trudges on.

When she arrives at the cowsheds, she may be frightened of something quite different: of the cow. She may be only a trainee, new at the job, and this animal is very large and bony, and seems to be provided at every corner with things that can hurt her. At some stage in her experience she is almost bound to learn that a kick can be very painful, and that a lash in the eye from the tip of a matted tail can be very painful too. Nor is it agreeable to be scolded in addition to your own pain, because you have let Buttercup, or Daisy, or Daffodil send a two-gallon bucket, nearly full, swirling away down the gutter. No use crying over spilt milk? I wonder how many hot tears have been secretly shed as the little trainee learned her task?

Some of them haven't stuck it. One girl went on strike, saying that she was allergic to cows, and would rather go through another London blitz than ever sit on a milking-stool again. That was that. But another one, a little Jewess from the East End who remarked that she scarcely knew what a cow looked like and had certainly never been so near one in her life, is more typical of those who have seen it through.

I think the credit which some of these girls deserve can scarcely be exaggerated. I really do. Heaven knows that I have sometimes wished I might never see a Land-girl again, as any WLA official would say if she were honest enough.

But how easily one's exasperation melts away! One is so much older than these children – for, after all, many of them are no more than seventeen or eighteen – and one should be more tolerant of faults for which they are not wholly to blame. I remember one particular morning when the siren woke me; I looked at my watch, six o'clock; it was January, pitch dark still; I lay listening to the planes overhead, then to the distant guns; then to a peculiar sound which, half-asleep, I didn't at first recognise but vaguely thought had some connection with the raid, then identified it as the familiar whine of the cooling-machine up at the cowshed, nothing sinister, nothing destructive, not a bomb or a shell coming down, nor even some horrible secret weapon functioning for the first time; no, just the old cooler starting up as usual; and I realised then that five girls (two of whom I knew to be frightened of raids) had already been in the sheds for an hour at their constructive task, getting the warm sweet milk, and I really don 't know whether I felt more ashamed of myself for being still in my comfortable bed, or for having ever been guilty of irascibility against these plucky and sturdy little toilers.

Then there are other jobs which go with the chosen profession of a milker. There is the dairy work, which entails amongst other things the monotonous business of washing endless bottles. There is the process known as mucking-out, which entails lifting the heavy, sodden, strawy litter and chucking it on to the mound outside – a mound which presently will be lifted again, in obedience to the beautifully economic arrangement of nature, and spread over the fields to restore what has been taken from them. Then the sheds must be sluiced down, the chocolate coloured water running unlovely away to add to the general dampness and chill. Not much of the novelist's sun-bonneted dairymaid here, when you come down to the real thing! Tess of the d'Urbervilles may have sat pressing her brow against the sweet-smelling flanks while a handsome young man courted her and the spurt of the milk-jets made a pastoral rhythm to the idyll, but the Land-girl knows that it isn't really like that.

There are other considerations which make the milker's job a particularly hard one, for instance the question of holidays. Every Land-girl, besides the annual holiday of a week and the public holidays to which she may be entitled, is supposed to have her Sundays free, and, except in special urgencies dependent on the season and the weather, a free half-day every week also. Besides this, it is considered right that she should have one completely free weekend in four, so that she can go right away from her work, to her home or wherever she chooses. Most Land-girls do get this, but in the case of a milker it is sometimes difficult to arrange. You cannot leave a cow unmilked; I have indeed heard some novices express surprise at the tiresome rapidity with which the animal fills up again. There was a horrible and haunting story of how the cows in France, abandoned by a peasantry in flight before the advancing armies, went mad with pain and discomfort and galloped distraught about the fields... But on a small farm, where the girl is perhaps the only milker, or on a farm where the dairy-herd is too numerous for the second pair of hands to manage alone, the problem of letting the girl off becomes very awkward. Solutions have been suggested, for instance, a 'pool' of trained milkers, living in a central hostel, who could be hired out in rotation to neighbouring farms; but many cautious farmers declared that nothing would induce them to risk a stranger bringing infection (principally of mastitis) into their herd, a very reasonable objection. Others felt apprehensive of gossip being carried round from farm to farm. It sounds absurd, doesn't it, when the need is so urgent and the best-intentioned plan being made by conscientious officials, to help both the farmer and his girl out of a difficulty? But this is what happens the moment you come up against human beings with their blighted experience. One can see their point of view. Outsiders mean talk, and talk means trouble. Goodness knows the insiders talk enough already, and squabble, and backbite, but at least it's all within the closed ring of the home-circle, and no doubt if it came to the point they would all cluster into defence against an outside attack. But don't let's have any strangers prying about, tale bringing and tale-carrying.

Any job involving human contacts can be very dis-heartening. So, perforce, the Land-girl is still often kept at work on the days when she should be free because there is no one to replace her. Her weekly wage goes up, of course, with the over-time rates on Saturday afternoons and Sunday, so that she is earning perhaps eight to ten shillings extra; but I wonder if she finds it sufficient compensation for the loss of liberty?

The Land Army and its Ministry are, however, not so easily defeated. They realise that the question is a serious one, not only for Land-girls at the present time, but also for dairy workers and farmers in the future; and with the co-operation of the farmers a solution will eventually be found.

It must bring some satisfaction to the girls who have

undertaken and stuck to this arduous job to know that they get a very high percentage of marks for it in the table of work-output which will be found on page 176 at the end of this book: ninety-one marks out of a hundred. And to the eternal honour of the Land-girl we must record the very large proportion who have been willing to go in for milking; a total of 20,159 in England and Wales (by September, 1943) or more than a quarter of the whole WLA, nor must we forget the milk measurers, girls with some experience of dairy-work, who have volunteered to take recordings at farms within their own area. This is responsible work, controlled by the Milk Marketing Board; special training is necessary, and a good deal of travelling about is involved, but the volunteer receives a weekly wage of £3 plus an allowance for expenses.

IX

General Farm-work, including Ploughing

She does general farm-work. A brief list of the jobs under this heading has already been given on page 45. Ploughing came first, for she has learnt to plough both with the tractor and the horse, and has indeed sometimes carried off the prizes in a competition over the heads of the men. But her general percentage of marks does drop a bit here, which is not surprising; the surprising thing is that she should have learnt to do it at all. Frankly, ploughing with the tractor is not a job for most women: that little iron seat is terribly exposed to the weather; it is terribly jolty ('Fairly shakes the inside out of you,' seems to be the current phrase when you press the question); it is terribly hard to start up the engine by hand on a cold morning – even a man with his superior strength and different construction finds it quite exhausting enough; and, even when you have got the thing going, the screwing-round of the steering wheel, time after time at the turn, all day long, perhaps on heavy clay, is an effort which in the opinion of many should not be required of any girl. Yet they do it. I remember meeting a girl who couldn't have been more than eighteen or nineteen; she was English, but she had escaped from Norway in order to join the WLA here. On the day I met her, she had been allowed to take out the tractor and the plough 'on her own' for the first time that morning. She was absolutely glowing with pride. I thought I had never seen anybody so youthfully excited or determined. 'Oh,' she said, 'when I saw those furrows stretching behind me, like the wake of a ship only brown instead of white, and knew I had done it all myself, I thought I should fall off the saddle with the thrill.' A good ploughing story comes from Devon, where on an isolated farm in the hill-country round Honiton, a London girl was set to plough for the first time a field with a slope of one in three. Not only was the ground coarse with bracken, but it was so steep that ploughing downwards was the only possible way, and even so the farmer, his wife, and small son had to hang on to the back of the plough to keep it in the ground at all. That girl had joined the WLA in 1939, and was fully capable of servicing her tractor. No doubt she had need to be, on that particular tilt of hill.

A Kent girl enjoys the distinction of being the first girl to plough by night. Not a moonlit night, when we have all grown accustomed to hearing the tractor travelling up and down till midnight or later (a strangely suggestive sound, I always think as I hear it, suggestive of the urgency of war, coming across the peculiarly resonant night-air, when all activity should normally be stilled and the labourers gone to their rest, and no sound heard but the cry of an owl or the bark of a fox), no, not a moonlit night, but a black night, when she had nothing but her own dimmed headlights to guide her. I wonder what that girl thought of, as she drew her furrows behind her? The enrichment of the imagination is so entirely a question of the person concerned: Did she think of her headlights as throwing a beam of hope across the future of the dark field, and of the furrows she couldn't see over her shoulder as the things which were to receive the growing seed? Or did she think of it merely as a job to be done, an over-time job, which would add some shillings to her weekly wage? Was it England she was working for, or her own pocket? Probably a mixture of both. She had sold stockings in a hosiery store before the war…

Women's marks, however, do drop on the average. Ploughing is a highly skilled job, and the standard of competition is high. She is coming up against men who have done it all their working lives. Still, she does not do so badly: she gets 65 for ploughing with horses, and rises again to 73 with the tractor, though she drops sadly when it comes to servicing the tractor as well as driving it – only 49 marks out of 100.

A report given by farmers judging at a Land Army demonstration may supply some useful hints to girls reading this book quietly in the evening after they have put their tractor away. It seems that many of them had no idea of proper lubrication, others did not even know where to put in transmission oil; others were unaware that the magneto should receive two drops of sewing-machine oil for every two hours running. (So was I.) Some, when asked how they left their tractors in winter, replied: 'Oh, we just put them away in a shed with a cloth over them and go home.' When what they ought to have said was: 'We drain the radiator with its head downhill, unscrew the radiator cap to prevent freezing on, and cover the engine with a rug or sack, and of course we leave it on paraffin not on petrol.' Some did not know the safe method of holding the starting handle, by keeping the thumb on the same side of the handle as the fingers, so that the hand is free to fly off in case of a back-fire. Correct air-pressure for tyres was not well understood, though this was attributed to the fact that most girls had

had experience of steel-wheeled tractors only. Considerable vagueness was displayed about the use of petrol as a fuel until the engine was hot enough to vaporise the TVO (tractor vaporising-oil). On the face of it, it would seem as though girls were not mechanically minded, but in fairness to them it was suggested that their employer hadn't the time or the patience to teach them. Employers vary: some can teach, and will; others can't, and won't. This, incidentally, has proved a great difficulty in organising proficiency-tests.

Their actual driving was much approved of. It was thought that some tried to drive too fast, and that others showed lack of judgement in trying to turn too short instead of taking a figure of eight; it was observed also that employers had not given enough advice on the setting of the plough. The net result of all this appears to be that only too often Land-girls will carry out what they have been taught to do, but that the majority lack the perseverance to gain extra information for themselves by asking questions from employers' uncommunicative by nature. They know what they do, but not why they do it. The one who will go a little further, the one who will take the extra trouble, the one who displays interest and curiosity, is the one who will come to the top, who will earn her proficiency badges, who will become a forewoman, and who in her post-war life is most likely to succeed, whether she remains on the land or returns to some other profession. There is an old French proverb which says, 'Help yourself, and Heaven will help

you.' Every young person embarking on life might well take that as a motto.

General farm-work means many dreary jobs. No one could pretend that weeding, hoeing, dung-spreading, or root-lifting were inspiring occupations. They are just jobs that have got to be done, and the Land-girl doggedly does them. Take root crops. This is a heavy job, and a wet one. Anybody who has walked a field of roots after partridges will know how wet it can be. The top leaves seem to hold water as nothing else holds water, except perhaps a pond. You are drenched to the knees after five minutes. The

Land-girl often spends her day among the roots, and if she is a girl on general field-work she doesn't necessarily get given a pair of gum-boots, rubber being in such short supply and gum-boots being reserved for the girls who are on what is considered the really wet work, such as swilling down the cowsheds or ditching. Personally, I think that every girl who is out amongst the roots or deep crops is better entitled to knee-high Wellingtons than the girl on the concrete floor of the cowshed, where her feet, but not the whole of her legs, need protection: wooden clogs would serve her nearly as well. The girl who works out in the fields has all my sympathy. Of all agricultural jobs, hers is perhaps the least showy and the most monotonous. Mangolds may glow as orange as fire in colour, but you cannot warm your fingers at them. Indeed, as you handle them, they seem the most slippery and frozen things ever grown by earth. Perhaps the little Land-girl who has been a manicurist in her past life remembers the well-kept hands of her languid pretty clients, dipping their finger-tips in a bowl of warm soapy water, softening the cuticle, and complaining meanwhile about the strenuousness of social life. So tired this morning! never got to bed till three a.m... couldn't wake up till ten...

The shop was centrally-heated, and hot water ran from chromium-plated taps into porcelain basins; fur coats hung on hooks; handbags, rings, and suede gloves lay littered about. Chatter and gossip floated from behind discreet curtains. The proprietor drifted from cubicle to cubicle with an appropriate compliment for every customer. Was this really life, once? Can it have been so? The Land-girl pauses for a moment in her work, straightens her back, pulls off her woollen glove, looks at her own hand, red, blistered, cold, with broken nails and grated skin... With a sigh, she bends again to her task. There are still two hours to go before she can break off to have a snack in the middle of the morning. Was her sigh at all ironical? One wonders.

X

Hedging

Brishing and laying hedges is a more agreeable, though scratchy, task. There is something about the clean slicing of the chopper which is very satisfactory, and it is satisfactory also to trim an untidy overgrown mess into some form by your own effort and with your own single pair of hands. There is the pleasure of art in it, and a sort of creation. You start on a tangle, and leave it a shapely thing. Also, you feel you are giving a chance to the young shoots which would otherwise get strangled by their elders – a pleasurable reflection, surely, to all youthful hedge cutters who have recently escaped from parental rule. It does give you a sense of power and direction, I think, to lay about you in a skilled way with your sharp tools, eliminating what is unnecessary, encouraging what is wanted, abolishing the old muddle, and making a good provision for future needs. I watched a Land-girl tackling a high wind-break hedge of thorn; she didn't know I was watching her; in fact, I felt I was taking rather a mean advantage; but if she had only known, I was doing nothing but admire the workmanlike way she set about it. That hedge must have been ten foot high, and the girl in the green jersey wasn't much over five foot, so that as she stood on the ground looking up and considering her task I thought of Jack and the Giant; she was quite alone, and she might have looked rather small and forlorn in the December landscape, but for a certain excitement in her eyes and a glow on her cheeks; and then she brought her step-ladder and propped it in place and started chopping; and next time I passed that way, a day or two later, that neglected giant of a hedge was beginning to look as though it had had a hair-cut. It had that closely-shaven look which is so ugly in men and so becoming in hedges. The hair-cut had gone only half-way along, but the half that wasn't yet done: showed up the difference with the half that had been done. It certainly did. Even a non-country-sighted person would have noticed that.

But, you may say, this is a rough job, this brishing, usually undertaken by rough labour without any thought of art at all; just a necessary yearly lopping to keep hedges in order. So it is. But there is another department of hedge-control in which Land-girls have specialised, and that is hedge-laying. The skilful laying of an old hedge is especially gratifying to the interested worker. You know that if it were left to shoot up into the air it would become merely thin and tall, with no bottom, and in course of time would become so meagre at the base that even the fattest sheep could squeeze through the gaps with no more loss than a single tuft of wool. It is within the power of the hedge-layer to correct and forestall this rank development – a fascinating art, once you have learnt it. You half-slice through the flexible stem, bend it down, secure it; and leave it, knowing that next spring it will start to shoot upward again from every joint, making a thick green barrier instead of a spindly useless towering fringe which serves no purpose save to screen the sunlight from the land. I have nothing but envy for the hedge-laying Land-girl, if she likes her job and takes pride in it.

A further advantage about hedge-work in general: it means bonfires. Now is there anyone with soul so dead that he doesn't respond to the charm of a bonfire? There must be something primitive in all of us that makes us cry out Oh! when we see a fire blazing in the open, and makes us want to rush to poke it into still fiercer flame; something atavistic in us, which goes back to when man first discovered fire – a moment of pride and power which we have subconsciously never forgotten. Besides, apart from this, there is an extraordinary beauty in the sight of flames out of doors, colouring the bleakness of the winter morning, and an extraordinary paler beauty also in the sight of smoke drifting across the fields, perhaps while a few stars and the belated moon are still hanging in the sky. The Land-girl on hedge-work has the enjoyment of the bonfire. True, she can't stand back and see it from a distance as we passers-by on the road can see it. But she does have the fun denied to us, of heaping a further fork-load of rubbish and hearing it crackle and seeing it blaze up...

No, I do not pity the Land-girl at work on our hedges.

XI

Haymaking, Harvesting, Threshing, Thatching

But what is to be said about her when she starts on haymaking and harvesting? Surely those are the romantic jobs of agriculture, sunburnt mirth and all that? Certainly they are neither grim nor dreary, and although they can be pretty strenuous it is perhaps preferable to be too warm than too cold. She has done well in this department. Her physical strength and endurance have been a surprise, for loading sheaves is a heavy test – she gets 61 marks for this, and 67 for rick-work with hay – 80 for driving the hay-mower; and in turning hay she seems to excel, for she gets 92 marks out of a possible 100. Stooking gives her 63, and rick-work with corn 64. With threshing she rises to 70; but both threshing and thatching, those jobs so closely associated with corn production, demand separate paragraphs to themselves.

With the enormous increase in arable land, threshing became an urgent problem, and the manning of the machines had to be provided for somehow. The demand was met in great part by the importation of girls from the North and the Midlands to the more southerly counties, girls from the cotton mills of Lancashire and the stocking factories of Nottingham, and no words can say how grandly they carried out the dirty noisy task. They arrived in their

hundreds at the southern stations, tumbling out of the trains with their bundles, cheerful, excited, filling the air with their broad North-country accents, exclaiming in surprise at the mildness of the climate, at the lush greenness of the softer country, at the unfamiliar appearance of Kentish oast-houses and warm gold-lichened barns, at the absence of moorland and at the rich water-meadows of Romney Marsh. 'Ba Goom!' one heard, as one drove them through the lanes towards their billets. It was like having three Gracie Fields in the back of the car. I don't know what they had expected to find, but at least one girl had been told by her mother to leave her false teeth behind, as she might get bombed down South. Many of them had never left home before, had never been outside Leeds, or Sheffield, or Bradford; and some of them, after the first excitement of finding themselves in what seemed to be a foreign country, grew horribly homesick. Some couldn't stand it, and went home; but the majority, although they might sometimes stand in tears amid the alien corn, stuck it. It was particularly hard on them because, their homes being so far away, they couldn't dash back for the respite of a weekend; and moreover they had no friends in this new neighbourhood. They minded this, the homesickness and the separation, more than they minded the work itself. In fact, they didn't seem to mind the work, they rather liked it on the whole; they didn't mind the constant clanking noise for they were accustomed to the noise of machinery; and they liked the odd change to the open air after the shut-in life of the factory. But they did mind this knife-cut through the strands of their affections.

They worked in gangs of four to a machine, and, unlike most Land Army occupations, threshing did offer a chance of promotion to the most competent girl. She could become the forewoman, which meant better pay and the responsibility of keeping the time-sheet and the wages-sheet. It gave her some authority over her comrades. One of the criticisms inevitably incurred by the WLA as opposed to the Women's Services, is that it offers so little scope for advancement to more enterprising and intelligent members. Obviously, you cannot become a sort of non-commissioned

officer or indeed any kind of officer, when you are an isolated worker and there is nobody else to command. Gang-work does at least supply this form of compensation as well as giving you some companionship in your work, and that is something to be said in favour of the threshing gangs; something which, heaven knows, they deserved and needed.

Thatching is another job in which women have proved them-selves useful. True thatching by hand is a dying art today, and even in peacetime the difficulty of obtaining the services of a thatcher was considerable, where no man capable of carrying out the work happened to be regularly employed in other capacities on the farm. The neat time-honoured thatch of good sound straw, pegged down and trimmed, was only too often replaced by an unsightly substitute of no more beauty than asbestos roofing: it might be serviceable, it might be labour saving, but it made our ricks look like huge white-paper parcels rather badly tied, and abandoned in the fields. Fortunately, a device like an enormous sewing-machine with a giant needle plocking up and down through the straw came to the rescue, and was found to be an implement most suitable for girls to work. Living in a caravan themselves, they trailed their machine from farm to farm, turning out perhaps a hundred mats of thatch in a day, and they were capable of setting it on the ricks themselves if required.

Taken all in all, the nation which has never gone short of a loaf owes much to the girls who have helped us to our unrationed bread. They have harvested our corn, kept it dry, and threshed it out when the time came. The verse printed inside their Christmas card, almost medieval in its simplicity, has a special application to them:

> *Be gentle when you touch bread,*
> *Let it not lie uncared for, unwanted,*
> *Too often bread is taken for granted.*
> *There is such beauty in bread,*
> *Beauty of sun and soil,*
> *Beauty of patient toil,*
> *Wind and rain have caressed it,*
> *Christ often blessed it.*
> *Be gentle when you touch bread.*

I don't know who wrote this, but I do know that it was a sudden jet of true poetry, and that the women who inspired it were poets, too, in their way, the hard way of patient toil, when they didn't know in the least that they were doing anything which could even remotely be called poetical; didn't stop to think even that they were putting the crisp loaf on the cottage breakfast-table; but knew only that they were dirty, tired, blistered, and that it was necessary for the job to be done.*

---

* Since writing the above, the author has been discovered to be Corporal F. Young, WAAF.

XII

Land-reclamation

Land-reclamation sounds a giant's task, but the diminutive Land-girl has tackled it. It is perhaps one of the best Land Army 'stories,' in the journalistic sense of the word. It comes from all parts of the country; from Devon, from Cumberland, from Durham, from Essex, from Romney Marsh in Kent. Look at the photograph of the girl with the big 'grab.' A most unfeminine implement. Then read the story behind one of these excavators, a story told on the wireless by one of the girls at the controls – she is aged nineteen. It concerns the widening and deepening of the River Skerne in Durham, a river which has always had a bad name because annually it floods and lays thousands of acres waste, along the thirty miles of its course .

'My grab works three or four times to the minute. A grab is a big shovel affair, with teeth, that digs into the bottom of the river and gouges out eight cwt. of soil and clay and stones at a time. Then back goes another of my levers, and up comes the grab. Another lever turns the whole excavator round; then I press a pedal with my foot and tip the whole lot out of the grab on to the top of the river bank, just where I want it.

'Soon I shall have to cross and start on the other bank. That's a whole day's job. You've got to tip enough stuff

into the river to make a bridge to carry the excavator across, then you've got it all to dig out again. But actually we are not simply scooping out of the river bed all the time. Making the bank straight and sure – what we call 'chamfering' – is just as important. We've got to see that this river is wide enough, as well as deep enough, to take all the drainage water that it should have been taking all along. That is why there has been this terrible flooding – just because the river was too sluggish and jammed-up and twisted and shallow to get the water away. So part of the time we hack away at the banks with the grab, and throw all the soil and clay well back. All this stuff goes to make a thick, low wall right along the river, in case it ever tries to flood again.

'As well as deepening and widening the bed, we've got to be always on the lookout for old drains that have been stopped up perhaps for hundreds of years. It never takes the men long to get them open – and that means that fields maybe half a mile away are starting to be drained at last. Then we've got to watch for obstacles like big boulders and trees; the men get the boulders out; we drag the trees out.

'I think it's a real man-size job, this. We start the paraffin engines ourselves every morning, then we just slog away all day. We do about sixty or seventy yards a day, and each of us shifts about 200 tons every day. This is supposed to be one of the biggest drainage jobs in the country and one of the fastest, too. If we carry on like this we should be through in another eight months. And when it's done, we shall have reclaimed about 60,000 acres for real safe cultivation.

'I had never done any work outside our house before, and Evelyn is only seventeen – two years younger than I am – and she worked in a shop. We both learned to drive tractors when we joined the Land Army, but we were surprised when the Machinery Officer for the county told us he was short of men to work excavators on this scheme, and would we like a week's training. Well, that was all the training we had – and what a shock they got there when two Land-girls came for training! Then we came back, climbed in, and got started; and we've done nothing else but this ever since.

'I wouldn't swop this job for anything; I really wouldn't. It does get a little monotonous at times; you don't do much travelling in an excavator, and you could get sick of seeing the old grab swinging up and round, round and down, all day long. But if ever I feel like that, I've just got to look down the river. All the way to Darlington it is now running freely in a deep, wide bed with safe banks, draining land that's never been drained before. And then I compare it with up-river, where we haven't reached, with its narrow, twisted banks sometimes only a foot above water level. Or I look round at the poor wretched fields round here – abandoned, covered with rushes, the soil so *cold* after the flooding that nothing else will grow. Next year I shall come along here and look at the crops of barley and wheat and I shall think, 'I had something to do with that. I helped to waken up *that* weary river!'"*

Another excavator is under the sole charge of a Land-girl who was once manageress of a gown department in a big shop. She is managing something very different now. She

---

* The extracts from this talk are reproduced by kind permission if the BBC.

and her particular monster are engaged in clearing and reclaiming Wragmire Moss in Cumberland, a 160-acre swampy stretch just south of Carlisle, which hitherto has resisted all attempts to transform it from a useless into a productive area. For myself, I like to feel that even in our neat little island Nature can still assert herself and will not allow herself to be entirely tidied up by the ingenuity of man. There is something in one which does not like the Skerne to be tamed and which prefers the wild moorland not to be regimented into row upon row of the obedient potato. But this is a personal point of view most subversive to the ambitions of the WLA and the Ministry of Agriculture.

Anyway, Wragmire Moss is being brought into line. The big scoop, operated by the Land-girl, brings out eight cubic feet at a time of dark, damp peat, thus creating a ditch which by the summer of 1943 was already two miles long. Italian prisoners finish off the clearance with spades, and the water now flows steadily along the new channel. Cultivation should begin before long, and should continue permanently long after the war emergency has passed.

Nazeing Common in Essex is being brought into line too. This is no swamp, but rough thistly ground, bumpy with emmet hills and of no practical use to anybody. A twenty-one-year-old ex-knitting-machinist and a twenty-four-year-old ex-typist, living together in a caravan, are responsible for the excavator on this particular track. Truly the war has precipitated young womanhood into some unexpected jobs...

A further dozen Land Army girls are working as excavator drivers for the Thames Conservancy Board.

In Cheshire, six thousand acres of the Frodsham and Helsby Marshes have been reclaimed. Six girls, whose ages range from seventeen to twenty-five, trained as excavator operators under the supervision of a foreman; and, with one machine to each girl, have cut great ditches to drain the rush of water into the Mersey.

The Fen country is a part of England towards which one's thoughts turn whenever the question of drainage comes up. Naturalists and sentimentalists may deplore the taming

of that unusual region, with its black soil, its wide skies, its dykes and ditches, its chain of mouldering churches, its reeds, its bird-life; I confess that I sigh myself. There is nothing else in England like it (except, on a smaller scale, Romney Marsh); and must this also be made to conform, to lose its personality? is Nature never to have her own way anywhere? Such regrets are, of course, quite idle. Clearly, wheat is more profitable than duck shoot rents, and we must school ourselves to read without a qualm about cement roads being laid and of Adventurer's Fen being dried out, the reeds and rushes being burnt, and stumps of bog-oak blasted from the peaty ground where they had lain buried for 2,000 years.

But perhaps the best land-reclamation stories of all come from Devon. Here it is not a question of swampy ground to be drained, but of tough moorland to be cleared – scrub, bracken, trees and tree stumps, and then the ploughing to be done, the crop to be sown and finally harvested. In some places the whole work has been carried out by Land-girls, the clearance, the first ploughing, the disc-harrowing, the second ploughing, the setting of potatoes, the ridging up. Bracken land has both its advantages and its disadvantages. On the credit side, it is rich in potash, and thus excellently suited to potatoes when once it has been got into order; but on the debit side it calls for expert technique especially in the first ploughing, which must be deep, ten inches at least, and then the making of the tilth will demand careful cultivation, usually with the disc-harrow. (A 110 girls, working for the Devon WEAC have entirely dealt with 1,300 acres of potatoes. That is to say, that they have ploughed, cultivated, planted, ridged, hoed, picked, clamped, and finally graded for market.)

XIII

Orchards and Fruit

If land-reclamation may fairly be called a specialised job, so may fruit-spraying and pruning. Spraying is one of the nastiest jobs on the land. Some farmers refuse to put women on to it and not always because they think they can't do it. I was amused by the answer one farmer gave me, 'No, I don't put my girls on to spraying,' he said, 'because I find that if the men think the girls can be got to do it, the men then refuse to go back to it themselves.'

It is not so bad in summer, when you do not need to be so thorough, i.e., it is sufficient 'to wet the leaves, blossom-buds, or young fruit; but in winter when every bit of the tree even to the extreme tips of the most out-of-reach twig must be covered, and when on a windy day the drift of the spray is apt to blow back into your face and all over your clothes, then you may well wonder why you ever joined the Land Army.

Pruning is interesting, if you take the trouble to approach it scientifically and not in a spirit of chop and lop. There is something very satisfactory in leaving a beautifully-shaped young tree, well-groomed, with plenty of space and light and air for every necessary growth to develop. It is interesting, because different varieties need different treatment, so, to the intelligent expert, there can be no monotony about it – and monotony is one of the most soul-destroying dangers in many agricultural pursuits. The most usual fault of beginners is that they prune too lightly; they do not realise what an amount of kind cruelty a tree will stand. Land-girls might take this hint to heart. The wisest amongst them will not despise a little book-theory in addition to their practical experience, though one must admit that most diagrams or even photographs in the handbooks seem to bear little relation to the problem that confronts one when faced with the tree itself. Those little lumps, oval or rounded, that were so obviously either leaf-buds or fruit-buds in the picture, do not seem nearly so clear as you peer at them along the branch. And Nature has failed to provide the convenient arrow showing just where you ought to shorten the maiden laterals... One comes to the conclusion, perhaps rightly, that half an hour's instruction out of doors with a knowledgeable pruner is worth three hours study under the lamp. But books do supplement, theoretically, all the same.

Fruit-picking, as opposed to spraying and even to the numbed fingers of winter-pruning, must rank as one of the pleasantest jobs on the farm. From the worker's point of view, much of it takes place in the best possible weather, meaning that it is neither too hot nor too cold. The soft fruit, of course, comes at the height of summer, and picking strawberries all day long with the sun beating down on your bent spine can become wearisome enough; but there is little to be said against work among the currants, raspberries, gooseberries. Cherries and plums fall due in the summer also, but, perched on your ladder among the branches of a leafy tree, you find some shade, and the only drawbacks here are that you may fall off the ladder (your own fault) or get stung by a wasp (not your own fault). But the best moment of the fruit-picker's season arrives with the pears and apples. Golden September, brown-and-blue October, two of the loveliest months in England's year. Many a town-girl, sensitive to such things, must have experienced a real revelation of beauty when first she found herself in the orchards heavy with fruit on some gold-dusted morning, and reared her ladder into the boughs and became an inmate of that strange jewelled world above the ground, where the citizens hang coloured and rounded among the flocks of leaves, waiting for the touch of her careful lifting hand. For they must not be bruised, these Coxes, these Blenheims, these Ribstons, these Ellison's Orange, these Laxton's Superbs, these Beauties of Bath; nor must the big cookers, Bramley's Seedling, Lord Derby, Newton Wonder, Peasgood Nonsuch, Beauty of Kent: an apple bruised is an apple lost. They must part gently at the spur or stalk, without twisting or tugging; and must gently be deposited in the basket slung at her hip. There is an art and a skill in all this; tenderness and rapidity must be combined. It is otherwise for the cider apples and the perry pears; they are the riff-raff of the orchard, and the more you bruise them

the better they be, or at any rate none the worse, for in any case they will be roughly heaped in mounds like miniature mountain-ranges, until the time comes for them to be flung into the press.

And once the fruit is picked, there still remains the grading and packing. One of the prettiest sights I ever saw was four Land-girls sitting on upturned packing-cases under an oast house in the warm September sun. They sat round a huge sea of Orange Pippins, and I don't know which were the rosier – the apples or their cheeks. It was just a harmony of complementary colours, in browns and reds and greens. The browns came pale in the wood of the boxes, the wicker of the bushel-baskets, the corduroy breeches, darker in the sunburnt hands moving amongst the fruit, and in the immense Mexican straw hats which for some odd reason two of the girls were wearing, giving them a startlingly foreign appearance in that very English farm-yard; the reds came in the apples and in the red-brown tiles of the roofs; the greens in the few leaves still clinging to the stalks, and in the familiar jerseys, so close-fitting to the young figures. The whole picture seemed powdered over with gold from the latening sun, late in the day as it was late in the year; and the laughter of the girls seemed golden too, if sound may be translated into terms of colour.

> 'Golden lads and girls all must,
> As chimney sweepers, come to dust'

These words came inevitably into my mind, but there was nothing of sad mortality in that scene; only a warmth and glow and richness of young life, with England at her loveliest and the waters of the defensive Channel sparkling not so very many miles away.

Grading may be largely a matter of common sense: you put the biggest fruits together, then the medium, then the smallest, throwing out the imperfect of whatever size. Packing demands some skill and practice. You must pack in layers, eye upwards, and then cheek upwards, and although your basket or box must be neatly full by the time you have finished, it must not bulge above the rim or other baskets or boxes stacked on top of it will result in bruising. Moreover all fruits must firmly touch, or they will shift about in transit, and bruising will again result. All these things have to be learnt by the Land-girl; and if she happens to be a London girl and economically-minded, she may remember going down to Covent Garden at some early hour when the market-carts had just crawled in from the country with their loads, the drivers fast asleep but the horses knowing their way; and seeing the vast stocks of fruit from some unknown, unvisualised orchard discharged into the murk of a London dawn, flowers and fruit all converging into an unbelievable patch of country life, as though a whole province had arrived suddenly into town, fresher and more real than all the buses and shops, but rather surprised to find itself in the soot and under the sheds of a city market, amid the rattle of drays and the competitive shouts of the Cockney buyers. Here, in the peculiar metropolitan beauty of Covent Garden, she may once have bought her pound of apples cheap, thinking no more of what had gone to produce them – the spraying, the pruning, the picking, the grading, the packing, the despatching – than she thought of the producing of the milk in the bottle already standing patient on her doorstep as she started out.

But she knows now.

XIV

Gardening

The Land-girl is also a gardener. Over 10,000 girls had chosen to go into horticultural employment before the majority of girls in private gardens had to be withdrawn in 1943 in order to satisfy the farmer's priority claim. They used to work on the understanding that at least two-thirds of their time should be devoted to food-production; the other third might be given to the flower-garden, provided the authorities were satisfied that the girl was really replacing a man. Many a market gardener and nurseryman, as well as many a private employer, has been thankful for this means of salvation. Doubtless many girls have been thankful too, for this occasion to take up a profession they might otherwise never have thought of. For gardening is surely an ideal profession for the woman who likes it. The work is not so heavy as to put too great a strain on her physical capacity; and in the more expert branches the possibilities and range of interest is really unlimited. We might even live to see a woman appointed as Director of Kew or of the Royal Horticultural Society's gardens at Wisley! and even apart from these crowns of the botanical world, a more moderate ambition should be well satisfied by rising to the position of forewoman in a big commercial nursery or to the position of head-gardener in one of the beautiful private gardens which are a glory of our country. There seems to be no good reason at all why a woman, given the intelligence, the interest, and the energy, should not thus aspire. Of course, these natural qualifications are essential, but among the 10,000 who went in for horticulture in a more or less Robot spirit, because they had to do something and gardening seemed rather less tough than anything else (also you were sure of your weekends, as you couldn't be in farming), among those 10,000 there are now many who have gradually grown inspired by a genuine love of the thing. And what a fascination that thing can be! It would be difficult to exhaust the possibilities or to walk all round the field of potential exploration. There is hybridisation to be considered, the production of new varieties; the trying-out of every kind of new experiment, whether in soil cultivation or the introduction of new plants from abroad – after all, somebody first grew the tomato and the potato in this country; somebody improved on the old lilac; Mr Cox raised his famous Orange Pippin from a seedling because Mrs Cox had tied a ribbon on to a sprig of blossom and why should we suppose that this exciting and truly creative process is at an end? Of course it isn't. A hundred years hence, if we could return, we might be surprised to find our gardens enriched by valuable vegetables and lovely blooms we had never seen before, quite as much surprised as those who lived a hundred years ago would be on a miraculous return today.

Perhaps I write with too much feeling, and few will catch the infection; but it does appear to be a career well worth considering to the girl who wonders sometimes what she will do with herself after the war.

One may suggest also that herb-growing might prove an agreeable and profitable occupation. I can quite well imagine a couple of friends setting up in a cottage with an acre or so of ground, devoted to the cultivation of herbs useful both to the kitchen and the dispensary. A delightful picture rises before me as I envisage this possibility; the orderly little garden smelling as aromatic as a hillside in Abyssinia, the bunches drying in the sun, the lavender spread out on huge sheets, a pair of doves cooing in a wicker cage... Would any candidates care to apply? I would gladly provide them with the acre rent-free, even two acres, if they would build the cottage.

Even setting aside the more delicate and expert work which might attract a minority, it has become apparent that women are particularly gifted in horticultural and allied occupations. This is the one branch in which women have gained a higher percentage of marks than men – a noteworthy fact. In commercial horticulture the woman-worker is awarded 106 for cutting flowers, 106 for bunching them, 101 for packing. In market gardening she gets 103 for pulling peas, 101 for runner beans, 96 for broad beans. Planting potatoes gives her 95 marks, planting brassicas 90. Fruit picking, which is really in the same line of country, gives her 100 marks for small fruit, 99 for plums, 95 each for apples and cherries. From all this we may fairly deduce that the girl can hold her own when it is a question of skill and neatness, and where the necessity for physical strength is not too strenuously involved.

And it is most encouraging to note the real enthusiasm which has been shown. Over 600 girls have taken the Correspondence Course in Horticulture, and a number have also entered for the examinations set by the RHS.

XV

The Shepherdess

We seem to have been working gradually downwards towards what would once have been called the more womanly jobs. Of all womanly jobs on the land, I suppose the shepherdess is the most traditional. Joan of Arc watched sheep; Bo-Peep lost them; Mary had a lamb.

> *She walks, the lady of my delight,*
> *A shepherdess of sheep.*

And indeed it is not to be denied that there is something very suitable and pleasing in the picture of a young girl holding open a gate for her slow flock to pass through. And as for lambs... Lambs are almost absurdly charming; and how tactful of them to appear just when the fruit blossom fluffs over their heads. They seem made for one another. But here, as in most other aspects of country life, things are not always quite so idyllic as they may appear to the week-ender from the town. The lambs which he watches at their antics in the orchard on a dappled spring day have probably been born during a snowy night, and what that means to the shepherdess may best be described in the words of one of them. She has been at the job since September, 1939, so she knows well what she is talking about. For the first year she worked under the shepherd, 'very kind and thoughtful; I never had an angry word from him.' That is nice to know. She goes on:

'The busiest time of the year is the lambing season, which generally happens to fall in the winter months and goes on until spring. This means tramping through sodden pastures or ground often covered with snow, tending the new-born lambs, and more often than not giving assistance to the mother in bringing her lambs into the world. Sometimes in lambing the mother dies, and her lambs are given to another ewe whose own lambs are dead. To do this we have to take the pelt of the dead lamb, tie it on to the orphan, and the mother recognises the scent of her own lamb and adopts the orphan as her own; by this ruse a lot of time and trouble is saved. But it isn't as easy as it sounds. Often these months are rather trying as one becomes very wet early in the day and has to carry on throughout the day with very little chance of changing.'

But to get the lambs safely born is by no means the end of the matter. Once you have undertaken the care of animals you very quickly discover that there is no end to the things which may go wrong with them, a fact not always appreciated by the uninitiated holiday-maker who leans his arms on the top bar of a gate and watches cows chewing the

cud under the lengthening shadows at the end of a golden day. These creatures, he thinks, have nothing to do but eat and ruminate and grow glossy and more productive. The rhythm of their life is beautifully simple; a little dull, perhaps, but invariable, and according to routine, and no worry. If he had charge of them for a week, he would find out his mistake.

Sheep are no exception. Our shepherdess speaks again:

'As the hot days of summer arrive, so do the flies which attack the sheep with a vengeance, laying eggs in the wool which very quickly hatch into maggots. Treatment has to be given quickly or the life of the sheep is doomed.'

I could add most unpleasant details about what these maggots will do to a sheep, and where they will get to, but I refrain.

Then there is foot-rot...

It all means constant watching. 'Shepherd' or 'Shepherdess' are pretty names, with pastoral associations in our minds, but it is not surprising, when you know something about it, that the farmer, a realistic man, is more likely to refer to his shepherd as his 'looker.' Looker, indeed. One could readily believe that he must spend his whole time, looking.

And of course there is the shearing and dipping, all part of the day's work. Struggling animals, greasy fleeces; then the ridiculous pale pink beast, scampering off after its release, still bewildered, and no longer resembling the woolly toy at all. A little smudge of blood perhaps, from a slight cut on the shoulder or the rump... And then, later, an equally struggling animal poked down into the dip by a sort of pitchfork. It's all in the day's work, both for sheep and shepherd.

Our shepherdess already quoted holds quite a good opinion of sheep on the whole, an opinion which may perhaps not be shared by any motorist who has ever tried to get past a flock in a hurry. But then he is coming up against sheep on the road, which, after all, is not their natural habitat. When confronted with the difficulties of mere Nature they seem quite able to cope effectively:

'Sheep are not the brainless creatures they sometimes appear. Flowing through one of our pastures is a tidal river. When the tide is down the sheep have a habit of straying on to the saltings, but as the tide rises these saltings are cut off from the mainland and eventually covered with water. On one occasion some ewes with their lambs had been grazing on the saltings oblivious of the incoming tide. When the water had reached their feet and gradually rose higher, the ewes had one of two alternatives, to drown or to swim for it. The ewes took to the water, the lambs climbed on their mothers' backs, and after much splashing reached the safety of the mainland.'

Well, as an experienced Land-girl says so, we must take her word for it. She is an observant person, evidently:

'You will notice how sheep always turn their backs to a storm or on scenting danger. The lambs always stand well behind the ewe who stands at bay, her head down ready to defend the life of her offspring.'

I can't say that I have noticed this myself; it always seems to me that they all turn tail and scamper helter-skelter in the most helpless fashion. But over a further point at least I do find myself in complete agreement:

'One of the main objects in the life of a sheep is to find pastures new. However good the fencing and hedging strengthened by wire-netting and hurdles, they somehow succeed in finding a way out.'

How true! How sadly true!

XVI

Rats

We come now to something very different, and those who dislike rodents had much better skip this section, but no account of the Land-girl's activities would be complete with a mention of what is euphemistically called pest-extermination. This may include rabbit-gassing and mole-trapping, but in plain English it usually means killing rats.

There are more rats in Britain than there are people. Every inhabitant of these islands could adopt one specimen as a pet, if so minded, and there would still be about five million left over. That gives one to think. Then, rats must eat to live, and so must we, and unfortunately rats like eating the same things as we do. They appreciate, for instance, the corn which we propose to turn into bread for our own use – a serious matter in war-time. One rat will eat one hundredweight of food in a year, so a simple calculation shows that our fifty million rats will eat two and a half million tons of food in a year. Something had to be done about it:

> *'Rouse up, sirs! Give your brains a racking*
> *To find the remedy we're lacking,'*

and something *was* done about it, but it was rather a surprise to find it done by the very people who were traditionally supposed to mount a chair and scream whenever they saw so much as a mouse washing its whiskers. They took enthusiastically to the training which would send them out armed with long-handled spoons and poison, and would enable them proudly to exhibit to the casual visitor a corn-sack filled with two hundred corpses; or to hold up a pole with dead rats tied by the tail all along it...

It was a very cunning enemy they had to deal with. Nobody who listened to a talk given on the wireless by Mr Bill Dalton will ever underestimate the intelligence of the rat again. Mr Dalton, who proudly styles himself Ratcatcher to the City of London, was brought up to the business 'just about as soon as he could walk,' and his ancestors have been at it for more than two hundred years. So he knows. And his opinion of the rat is very high. He fights him, but he respects him. A rat, he says, has the sense to camouflage himself by hiding behind his own shadow; the glint of his eyes is the only thing that betrays him. If he runs up a pipe, he will always get on the side nearest the wall, so that if you hit at him you hit the pipe first. Then, he won't go near any piece of electricity plant which is dangerous; humans, says Mr Dalton, rather contemptuously, have to be warned in red letters. Rats know without any warning, just as they know better than to eat another rat which has died of poisoning. Yes, he respects the rat; and like the vast majority of Britons he is also beautifully humane – one of the marks of real

civilisation. He has never forgotten one of the first things his father ever said to him and his brothers, 'Never be cruel to a rat, he's one of the world's creatures, he may be a rat but he can't help it.'

There is one point, however, on which Mr Dalton goes wrong: he retains the old-fashioned idea about what he calls 'the female section' of the population. He is basing his opinion, apparently, on what happens in a factory when rats get into the canteen. Production is held up at once, as the girls immediately leave their machines. Well, Mr Dalton may be right about the factory, but it is evident that he has never come across the pest-exterminators of the WLA If he could tear himself away from his City of London, and spend his next holiday on a farm, he might perhaps revise his views and even discover some kindred spirits.

Once a Land-girl has taken to this work, it appears that nothing will induce her to give it up. Is it perhaps because, having overcome her original repulsion, she finds a particular delight in revenging herself upon her natural enemies? It would take a psychologist to answer that question. The net result is that about a thousand volunteers are employed by the County Committees and that they tour the farms with real gusto. They come from the most opposite kind of employment. A tap dancer, a waitress, a hairdresser, are amongst them. I have seen them arriving in their little car, the excitement of the hunt in their eyes, their pots and pans on the seat behind them, their sacks and spoons ready, looking like the complete outfit for a detective story. 'What have you got in there?' one asks rather doubtfully. 'Arsenic,' is the reply. 'And in there?' 'Zinc-phosphide.' It all sounds very sinister, and rather like a thriller-story about a particularly cold-blooded calculating murderer, 'The first day you put down bait, but the rat takes no notice; the third day you put

down fresh bait, and the rat becomes interested; the fifth day, you put down the poisoned bait...' There are nasty little details, too, which have to be studied; for instance, you have to learn to distinguish the rat's tail-trail from the rabbit's: the rat's long, stringy tail will wear the runway smoother; in trapping, you have to gauge the exact spot where the rat will land as it jumps the last stage of its run down a bank; you have to know exactly how much earth to put over the trap, enough to camouflage it and yet not too much to prevent it from going off. The rat-catcher, in fact, has to be a blend between the detective and the murderer. She has to track down the criminal, using a hundred different clues – the empty husks, the tunnels in ricks, the tail-trails across the heaped-up grain – and then has to turn him into being her prey. It is reported, however, that the skill displayed by the girls has been widely appreciated by all except the victims.

They train for the most part at county centres, and get instruction in the whole science, from the simple old method of working with traps or terriers to the more up-to-date methods of gas and poison. Gassing and poisoning are the most effective; in Devon, for instance, twenty-four thousand rats were caught by trapping, but nearly a hundred thousand destroyed by the other system. The details do not make pleasant reading for the squeamish. It is not pleasant to read about a bait which affects the lungs and makes the dying rat come out of its hole for air, nor of the 'splendid results' achieved by the administration of two doses of this bait followed by zinc-phosphide. It reminds one only too horribly of some Air Ministry communiques about well-concentrated bombing... Nor is it pleasant to read of the knacker's yard, where the rats had grown so numerous and so bold that they would come out and gnaw the carcases that were actually in process of being flayed...

But there are times when it is no good being squeamish. In the fight for life one must be realistic. And in the struggle between humans and rats it is a question of 'You, or us.' One would, of course, prefer to have a Pied Piper who might lead them all away,

> *Great rats, small rats, lean rats, brawny rats,*
> *Brown rats, black rats, grey rats, tawny rats,*
> *Grave old plodders, gay young friskers,*
> *Fathers, mothers, uncles, cousins,*
> *Cocking tails and pricking whiskers,*
> *Families by tens and dozens . . .*

but there was no Pied Piper available, and he functioned in Germany, anyway. There was, however, the Land-girl luckily for our food-supply.

XVII

Trees

We have left to the last a most important branch of the Land-girl's work: forestry. It should here be explained that there exists a special section of the WLA known as the Timber Corps. Ordinary members of the WLA are also employed by the Forestry Commission in nursery work connected with the planting and cultivation of young trees, but the heaviest and also the most expert work is undertaken by the Timber Corps. They number about 6,000; roughly 4,000 in England and Wales, 2,000 in Scotland. They wear the same uniform as the WLA with the difference of a green beret instead of the brown felt hat, and a special badge with a fir-tree surmounted by the royal crown, and the words TIMBER CORPS, WLA, written round it. The tree instead of the wheatsheaf... though the crown, the service, and the devotion are the same.

These girls are recruited and enrolled by the WLA in the ordinary way, and then sent for four weeks training to one of the camps established by the Home Timber Production Department of the Ministry of Supply. They might be sent either to Culford in Suffolk, or to a mountainside in Wales.*

---

* At the moment of writing, February, 1944, these camps are discontinued; but that is how it used to be.

There is plenty of change of scene in the Timber Corps, as will presently become apparent from some accounts given by the girls themselves. There is variety of occupation too, as we shall also show, and after the first week of their training the volunteers are allocated to special training in the branch of timber production to which they seem most suited. At the end of the training, if all has gone well, the volunteer is registered as a member of the Timber Corps, and may be drafted either into the direct employment of the Ministry of Supply or of a timber merchant who is engaged on work for that Ministry. The general welfare and supervision of members of the Timber Corps is controlled from a central office of the Ministry of Supply in Bristol, which employs a number of regional women officers for this purpose. Neither the WLA County Offices nor the local representatives take any responsibility for the welfare of the Timber Corps.

The woods of England are so little comparable in size with the vast forests of Russia, Germany, France, or Scandinavia, that in those countries they probably would not be dignified by the name of forest at all. But to us the names of our forests are dear; they have a romantic and historical association in our insular hearts: Sherwood Forest, the New Forest, the Forest of Dean, Savernake... And apart from these major names, how dear to us is the ordinary wood, its own name known perhaps only to the local people, but collectively meaning something inseparable from our picture of our country; those woods of which we believe – and how rightly – that there is no lovelier sight than the drift of their bluebells, and nothing nobler than the ancient oak. Who is so sophisticated, so urban, that he can walk unmoved down a ride in spring, under the youth of beech and chestnut, moss beneath his feet, veils of anemone around him, and the scent of the hyacinth in the air? Who so material of spirit, that cannot discover somewhere in the recesses of his heart a regret at seeing this perfection so despoiled, so torn? I have spoken with woodmen, picking up their wedges in the sudden silence that follows the fall of the tree, a silence broken only by the small cracking of twigs as the weight settles, and always have got from them the admission, gruffly given as they spat on their hands and prepared for the next bit of the job, 'Never do care, somehow, to see him come down.'

Apart from the sounds of war, there are in fact few more distressing sounds than the long rending crash of a fine tree being thrown in the wood; and among the sad sights of modern life one may number. The funeral procession of the mighty trunks, the living moss still green on them, the flat cut still freshly pallid where the boughs have been lopped. Chained to the long truck, they drag behind the tractor on their dreary journey, naked where they should have been leafily clothed, severed where they should have been rooted, humbled and horizontal when they should be proud and perpendicular. That is the tragic thing about a felled tree:

the complete reversal of all its natural intention. It is being forced to do the exact contrary of everything it was meant to do. It was meant to stand up, not to lie down; it was meant to have a great spreading head, in which birds could sing and nest, and the wind blow; it was meant to stand so firm in the earth, through centuries longer than many generations of men, that nothing but another natural force, a gale, could uproot it.

> *Woodman, spare that tree!*
> *Touch not a single bough.*
> *In youth it sheltered me,*
> *And I'll protect it now.*

In past years there was a certain dignity and beauty, as well as tragedy, three things which mix well together, in the sight of a great tree being taken away by great horses; they matched one another, in some suitably natural way; the rounded strength of the horses was somehow consonant with the rounded majesty of the trunk. The horses were polished and shiny, not rough as was the bark, but there was something of the same quality in both, which made the dragging away of the tree less humiliating somehow than this mechanised removal on lorries, this easy defeat of the strong, the old, and the beautiful, by something stronger, newer, and far less beautiful than the glossy team.

But one couldn't, and shouldn't, expect those whose

business is timber-selection or timber-felling to feel that way about it. If they did, they could never bear to do the things their job entails. As in rat-catching, you cannot afford to be squeamish: rats must die, and trees be thrown. It is no good being sentimental about it. Poison the rat, and cast the tree. Necessities of war make both things urgent.

Taking the utilitarian not the sentimental point of view, one must admit that the Timber Corps girl has done an astonishingly good piece of work. It is all the more astonishing because it is so varied. Let us make a list of the different things she does:

(1) She works in the forest itself. This means a variety of things. It means that she fells trees, measures them, hauls them – look at the pictures. It means also that she lops and trims, clears the ground, and assembles and burns the rubbish in grand bonfires on a winter's day.

(2) She works on the sawmills. This is a terrifying task, as anyone who has watched the great toothed circular saws whirring with murderous speed and sharpness will agree. It is a task which requires extreme care, precision, and concentration, for the saw which will travel with prolonged and undeviating ruthlessness up the solid trunk of wood will slice in one second through the soft finger, the pulsating wrist... Men have been known to shake their heads and say no, it didn't take their fancy; but the girls of the Timber Corps have done it.

(3) She is made responsible for 'acquisition.' This means that she goes round the woods all over the country, selecting trees which must be sacrificed to the country's needs. In order to check how much was available for war-production, a census of standing timber had to be taken in a great hurry. This was where the trained measurers

of the Timber Corps got their chance. Before the war, almost all the vast quantity of wood required by the coal-mines (pit props) came from overseas; and this was only one requirement amongst many. Before the war, the comparatively small job of obtaining home-grown wood, estimating its value, and negotiating with the owners, was done by men; but their place has now largely been taken by the women, skilled not only in examining and estimating the volume and species of timber standing in a wood, but also, in many cases, carrying the whole negotiation through from start to finish, including the drawing up of the contract, often a protracted matter calling for the maximum of patience and tact.

(4) She becomes a pole-selector. This also entails a great deal of travelling about, a great deal of walking, and long days spent in the woods. Telegraph-poles, ladder-poles, etc., for which there is a large and continuous demand, were previously supplied almost entirely by import, but during the war our own woods have had to meet the demand. In order to do this as economically as possible and to ensure that no suitable tree should be used for any other purpose, trees that are likely to be useful as poles have to be specially marked before any wood is felled. And not only do telegraph-poles and ladder-poles, as necessary in peace-time as in war, have to be supplied; but also that entirely novel necessity, the obstruction-pole for our road blocks. At the time

invasion threatened us, this need suddenly reared its head very urgently indeed. The English woods must do their part in hindering the enemy from surging down the English lanes... The work of pole-selecting has been taken over, almost exclusively, by the Women's Timber Corps.

(5) She becomes a measurer. This occupation is perhaps best described in the words of one of them, working with another girl as her partner:

'Measuring involves the holding of a long tape along the length of the tree and the encircling of the centre girth with another tape. In muddy weather, whichever of us does the girthing is the unluckiest. If you ever try walking round a log which is coated with mud you will know what I mean; but if you go one step farther and try to place a tape round its middle, I advise you to wear your oldest clothes. My 'other half' shares my daily life, and between us we cope with the office management of the mill and are responsible for the entire measuring of the incoming and outgoing timber. We share a small wooden hut in which we struggle with division, subtraction, and addition, brew weak tea and eat queer sandwiches. In the summer it is a grand life, but in the winter it is no good leaving your sense of humour behind.

'Not a spectacular job, ours? Perhaps not, but we have fun, and we know we are doing really essential work.'*

---

* Reprinted by kind permission of the Editor of *Woman*.

The writer of that article is now Measurer-in-charge at a New Forest mill, run by the Home Timber Production Department of the Ministry of Supply.

The foregoing list may have given some idea of what the Timber Corps has done and is doing, but these sketchy notes should be amplified by those who know best: the girls themselves. Lumberjills and pole-cats, as they are irreverently known, seem to have a gift for describing their experiences in a vivid and entertaining way. Land-girls don't usually seem very ready to express themselves on paper – a Welfare Officer of the ATS to whom I once made this observation, made the thought-provocative reply that it was true not only of Land-girls but of all the younger generation, so far as her experience went, largely because the spoken word meant more to them than the written word, thanks to the wireless, the telephone, and the talkies. I daresay she was right; but if so, it offers a pretty lugubrious future to those who still esteem English prose as a medium. Oh brave illiterate new world? This lack of familiarity with the pen has its charms sometimes: many girls ask for 'passionate leave,' and the County Offices are well accustomed to receiving letters which begin: 'Dear Madman.' The denizens of the woods, however, whether it is because they live in surroundings whose beauty really moves them or for any other reason, do not appear to share this inhibition with their contemporaries.

The following letter is long, but it gives so clear and racy a picture that we will not apologise for putting it in:

'I well remember the jeers of the old-timers at my first felling effort. After about a quarter of an hour my tree looked as though a rat had been gnawing it, and the next morning I did not know whether my head, back, tummy or arms ached the most. Our chief excitement was the putting out of forest fires. We had some very bad ones, as 1940 was such a dry year, and the young plantations only needed a spark to set them ablaze. Often we were out at night, once being called out to a fire miles away, and as quickly as we got one fire under control, the Germans dropped incendiaries in other places. At one fire I remember the ground being so hot with burning embers, that we were taking a boot off and holding it up in the air to cool a bit and standing like a stork, on one leg. The plan for having pole selectors was started in October, 1940, and I put my name down as a volunteer. The DO interviewed us, and asked us our reason for wanting to go. I said 'for adventure,' and got the job. First we went to the Forest of Dean for some training in this work and the chief pole man from the GPO took us around the woods, at other times we were having lectures at the College, and most of us muttering the Latin names of trees when we met each other. When the time came for us to start the most important and unknown job of pole-marking there was great excitement. Miss Tuffield and I were sent to Exeter. When we arrived at the office, no one really knew what to do with us. Had we got a car, because the work involved much travelling and walking? We had no car, so we were finally given a small plan of a wood near Chard and so got going. Our first task was to get most of our things packed in parcels and sent home, we just kept changes of underclothes and uniform, but after three weeks, in which it rained every day, and the difficulty of getting things dried, we had to have some things sent back to us. Our next job was at Oare. We were to contact a foreman who lived at Brendon, so we set out, but only managed to get as far as Porlock where we had to put up for the night. We just got a last room at a hotel there. We were asked if we wanted dinner, as our funds were so low we dared not have any, but asked for bread and cheese and tea. The girl there said would we have it in the bar or dining-room, as we were wet. Miss Tuffield said the bar, but I said the dining-room, so the dining-room it was. There I realised my mistake for the other guests were all in evening dress, and let us know how disgusting it was to let the Land Army in their hotel, and two left their dinner and went out, we could have eaten it, we were so hungry. The next day we were up and out before we offended them again, and as there was no bus until 4 p.m. we walked all the way. First we could not get to know the way. Nobody knew anything, so we trudged on. There were no signposts anywhere, and it was still raining. We got to Oare finally, and were told Brendon was five miles away. We got into another farm-house. Here we had no hot water for five days. When we got enough courage to ask for some we were given a half pint jug between us, and when the flannel was put in the water disappeared. We thought the job of pole-marking was not such an adventure after all. The DO at Exeter thought at this point that we should have a horse each, but the thought of asking for lodgings and rations for horses as well as for ourselves was a bit too much. After doing various woods in this division we were sent to the New Forest, and here it was still raining most of the time. I did not know the Forest was so big till we started to walk through it. Twice we got lost, and my friends from home sent me a compass. We started trying to take short cuts and found ourselves miles from where we should have been, we could not do much hitch-hiking there, but by this time we were getting used to roaming and beginning to enjoy it. We came in for some of the raids on Southampton and were always thankful to see everybody turn up safely in the morning. We had eight lodgings in different towns in the Forest and reckoned we walked 600 miles. Of course it must be realised that we are walking all the time we are working, and when you get into say 50-acre woods and have to explore from one end to the other, going up and down the lines of trees, one can soon cover a few miles. We found several dead ponies in the Forest that had been killed by bombs, often saw the lovely deer running, and once came in for a shooting day, when the keepers were out for venison. We had our most interesting work and time in North Wales. We had all our instructions by post, just a plan of the wood and the nearest station being given. Often we were sent to some unpronouncable place, most of them only had a bus on market day, one place we got to had one bus a month on Fair Day. These places might be anywhere up to twelve or fifteen miles from the station, but we managed to survive. The houses were miles apart, and Mrs Jones would tell you to try Mrs Hughes just over the mountain, and when you got to Mrs Hughes she did not take hikers. We got ourselves an AA Handbook which gave us the market days, and if we could we tried to move on those days. Of course we should have had a car, it would have saved much heart burning, wasted time, and shoe leather. We had to go from Bala to Lake Vyrnwy, which was twelve miles. To do this we took a taxi for seven miles, went about fifty miles by train, and then had to get down to the lake which was three and a half miles from our lodgings. There was a gang of Ministry of Supply men working there, so we got a lift to work, but still had about four miles each way to walk round the lake to get to the bit we wanted. We were on the road that was used once a month, when a bull chased us, we both broke the speed record, and the bull got stuck in a hedge, but we were frightened of bulls for a long time. We were staying at Llanavmondyffryncaeriog once when in Wales, and as we were coming back one night, everybody we passed, farm hands, boys and girls and women all informed that there was an important letter marked urgent at the post office. At one bank the lady looked at our books, and started saying, ' I see you've been to Bala and Stoke-on Trent and Shrewsbury,' and went all through to see where we had taken money out or put it in, but when she started telling the next person who came in to do business we thought it was time to depart. One day we could not find the wood for which we were looking and, seeing an old man, we asked him if he knew where it was. He said, 'No indeed, and you be aliens,' he said, but we tried to tell him we were only the Land Army. 'No,' he said, 'you be parachutist, Germans. I'll be fetching the police to thee,' so he went off and so did we, in the opposite direction, with our map and speech and everything. We rang up the Acquisition Officer, who when we explained the map, gave a good Welsh swear word and said the arrow on the road was the wrong way round and we had walked eight miles from the wood. Sometimes we moved three times a week. One day we would be in Aberystwyth, the next in Stoke-on-Trent, three days later at Devil's Bridge and our next move to Stafford or Worcester, and every time all our belongings had to go with us. All the porters and guards knew us at Shrewsbury station and would always take our luggage over for us. We went to the YMCA on Shrewsbury station as the refreshment room was not opened, and were informed before a crowd of ATS and WAAF that they did not serve the Land Army. So far we have had 232 different billets, and most of them jolly good, and we can always go back. I have to have at least 200 holidays when the war is over. Once a foreman was instructed to get a billet for us but he forgot all about it, and when we arrived in the pouring rain (as usual) no foreman, no billet. When we got hold of him he told us to wait in the village shop, and after three-quarters of an hour came back and said he had found us a lodge for one night and would move us the next day. We were shown into a dirty room, which contained a rusty stove and a wheelbarrow, and he told us that would do us for the night. We were so hungry that we got some rations from the shop and some wood and borrowed two cups from the young man's landlady. She brought us an orange box with a piece of newspaper for a cloth, so we had our meal, but decided we could not stay the night there, but would go to the next village. We asked the lady how much we were in her debt and she thought it was worth 5s. each. We spent one night at a place in Staffordshire in a police cell. Bed and eggs and bacon 1s., so what we lost in Wales we gained in Staffs. We walked to Llangollen once for eight hours for lodgings, and finally got in if we would share a room. We said yes, of course, thinking she meant us two, but when we went to bed there were nine of us there. On the Saturday we both had a bath, and when we were having dinner in the cafe attached to the place the good lady comes in and enquires in a loud forbidding voice of the forty or so people dining there, 'Who had a bath?' In a very small voice Miss Tuffield said, 'I did,' and me 'I did,' and are informed that it is not a hotel. At Devil's Bridge we stayed in a hotel on conditions we must live in the kitchen as they were short of staff. Of course we agreed, and said we would help wash up. We did for all the other guests and farm hands and it amounted to an hour and a half of work, my friend thought it time to finish and dried her hands and went, but the good lady called her back and told her she had not done the saucepans.

'At the beginning of 1942 we were called to Shrewsbury in a hurry, and were told that we were to start a new work, the taking of a census of all the woods and forests in the country; our part being Division 2 and some surrounding parts. This was something very new, we were to go with a census officer and measure with him. We did not know much about hard woods as our work had been amongst soft wood all the time. We had to mark out acres and parts of acres, walk all over the woods – one was 900 acres – till I thought my legs would give out. Most of the work was done with snow inches thick on the ground. We worked Shropshire, Worcestershire, Staffordshire, Warwickshire, Cheshire, then went over it again. Next we went to Dorset and Wiltshire, finishing off someone else's part. On every map we did one mile of hedgerow timber, starting from the south in the middle of the map to north. A dead straight line across hedges, fields, ditches and anything else that came in the way. There were, I think, about eighty of these maps.

'We saw the most beautiful country which is England as no one else could possibly have seen it. Once we were had up by the police as suspicious-looking characters going into woods with maps, etc. It took us five months to do all this work, which as you can imagine took hours of office work when the day's work in the woods was over. When we got back to Shrewsbury we were very disappointed to hear that we were no longer pole-selectors for them, as they had promised that our job would be there when we had finished the census, for they told us we must just do ordinary measuring for the rest of our time. However, Bristol gave us a transfer to a private firm to be pole-selectors for them, and off we went to a place near Hull. Here we were put to stripping bark from poles for the duration and a big drop in our wages. Of course we did not like it, for one thing the work was too heavy, once we were asked to move 81 telegraph poles three times. After four weeks we were transferred to Division 4. We were met at Reading by a works officer, whose first question was, could either of us drive, we could not do the job here without a car, there was one waiting for us, and we would have it in two weeks time. We thought we had come to heaven, but that was seventeen months ago, and we are still walking. We found difficulty in getting paint here and could not get the office to send us permits. They suggested sending a large amount, and us taking it around. Do they know how heavy paint is and how messy?

'I am sure forestry work in its all is the most interesting of war jobs. If you were at it till doomsday there would always be something new to learn. Some of the difficulties were getting boots repaired, washing done, our mail delayed sometimes for weeks. Estate owners and agents have been a great help, not to mention lorry drivers for the lifts they have given us. It is New Year's Day, 1944. A year, I hope, of promise. That the Timber girls will all do their share in getting the war finished, and promise for all the world of such a time that has never before been known, freedom, love and service for all.'

(*Signed*) D. E. BELLCHAMBER

It will have been observed that these two young ladies were sometimes regarded with suspicion by the local inhabitants. This seems to be the usual lot of those who go prospecting for timber. A pole-selector writes: 'Pole-selecting is one of the jobs the Land Army seem to know nothing about, judging from the interest my partner and I have excited on the rare occasions of our meeting them, but our bicycles, equipped with paint-pot, calipers, bill-hooks, knapsacks, etc., are now well-known in many districts where we have at first been regarded as an advance party of the invasion. We have never yet been successful in removing the rooted idea in people's minds that we actually climb trees to find out their height.' This correspondent does not consider pole-selecting a strenuous job; accommodation has been a difficulty, and they have lodged in anything from a four-roomed cottage to a mansion; sometimes they have got a crick in the neck from looking upwards at all kinds of trees in the hope of finding a straight one for a pole; they have suffered from chilblains in winter and mobile haloes of flies in summer; but 'we love our work and wish only that other members of the WLA could have the same opportunity of being able to enjoy the beauties of the different counties.'

Another excellent letter will be found on page 139 in the section dealing with the Timber Corps in Scotland.

These girls, like other members of the Land Army, have been recruited from many different kinds of occupation. It is not surprising to hear from one of them that 'we never thought we would be able to tell one tree from another at first.' (This particular girl is now Forewoman in charge of nineteen men and eleven girls.) One girl comes from Jamaica, and was a professional singer. Another, who is a married woman with three children, was a musician and music-teacher; interested in sociology, she also had experience of clinics, clubs, and Women's Institutes; was a lecturer in music, history, and English literature, also on goat-keeping. Her experience in the woods has been almost as varied as her experience in pre-war life, for she has done lorry-driving, cord-wood cutting, cross-cutting, burning, measuring, stacking, and office-work in the mills. Evidently not finding this sufficient, she also has eleven workers billeted on her; finds time to offer her services for a job after the war ('Having become a member of the Timber Corps, I would like to see its fortunes through to the finish') and ends up by remarking rather wistfully that her real hobbies are hunting and sailing, but that she 'hasn't time for them now.'

Yet another was engaged in forestry during the last war, and is now back in it, felling timber – as a grandmother.

And lastly, there is a poet. A poet in a forest – what could be more suitable?

> *What care I if eight-inch snow*
> *Makes walking wearisome and slow?*
> *Sepia are trees and rocks and windswept ground,*
> *Sepia the distant crag, the wall of stone.*

All else is white – snow whiteness lies around,
Intense, unsullied, over slope and mound,
My chain of footprints breaking it alone.
And wheresoe'er I turned my pleasured eyes
A living etching spread before me lies.

The other poem which she gives me permission to quote has nothing to do with forestry, or with the WLA either, but I feel that it should go in, if only to prove her claim to that proud title, and to prove also what the Land-girl can accomplish in spheres not particularly her own:*

What I have, I am. What I possess
I do become, incorporate in me.
Have I a friend, I am one; have I foe
Straightaway I do become an enemy.
Do I enslave another, then am I
More abjectly a slave even than he
Being slave of my own making, but I am
Free if all things I own have liberty.

I will not be imprisoned, chained. I'll own
Only the lark on the wing, the dove in tree.
Alas – I own the world, and so am bound
Until all quarters of the world are free.

---

* With acknowledgements to Miss Hebe Jerrold.

XVIII

The WLA in Wales

This small but extremely beautiful region of our island must be considered separately, for in many parts of Wales conditions are very different from those obtaining on the average English farm. In some Welsh counties, such as Pembrokeshire, which are occupied largely in dairy-farming, the difference is not so great, but in the hills and remote places you could readily believe that you had travelled away to some foreign country. For one thing, there is the language. We have all grown accustomed to hearing Welsh on the wireless, but perhaps most English people, who don't happen to have spent their holidays in Wales, haven't realised that Welsh is by no means a 'literary' language, kept alive by the Eistedfodds or by patriotic societies, but is the very living and everyday language of the people. I think that to many of us it may come as a surprise on a first visit to hear the children chattering to one another in the streets.

This, as one may well imagine, constitutes a very real difficulty to many of the Land-girls who have been drafted from England into Wales to supplement the number of Welsh girls working in their own country. It is not an insuperable difficulty, for the majority of Welsh people are bi-lingual, and consequently it is possible for the Welsh farmer to give his Land-girl his instructions in a language which she can understand. But when she finds herself surrounded by a crowd of fellow-workers and neighbours all happily jabbering together and totally unintelligible to the poor stranger – and Welsh people are far more voluble as a rule than the somewhat tongue-tied English – she must feel herself very cut-off indeed. The Land Army authorities, in this as in other matters, are sympathetic and reasonable: they don't try to retain an English girl against her will, for the policy of the WLA has always recognised that an unhappy volunteer is worse than no volunteer at all. But such cases are not frequent; the girl usually manages to adopt herself somehow. She probably ends by picking up some words of Welsh, even if it is only to address the animals under her care, the animals not being bi-lingual as their owners are.

Another difference to which the English girl has to adapt herself is, that the Welsh farmer is usually more thrifty than the English and that his standard of living is consequently less high. But this is the kind of thing to which any sensible person very soon becomes adjusted. One forgets one's original standards with astonishing rapidity, and takes the new conditions quite for granted.

The greatest difference of all, however, lies in the very nature of the country. England, generally speaking, possesses a gentle, even a cosy landscape; with the exception of the North Country fells and the moors of Yorkshire, Devon, and Cornwall, it is essentially undramatic; it is neither bleak nor desolate nor wild; it is thickly populated, richly cultivated, and even on the most isolated homesteads the sense of modern amenities is never far distant. In the hills of 'Wild Wales,' as George Borrow called it, things are otherwise. You might be not only in another country but in another century. For those who appreciate this opportunity of escape from the high organisation of modern civilisation – and such unusual people do exist, even today there is an unspeakable charm in getting back to more primitive conditions, to a rougher and more individual life, led in surroundings of extreme natural beauty. You have, admittedly, to possess a somewhat romantic temperament; you have to prefer the rushing torrent, the magnificence of mountain solitudes, the emptiness of the long valley, to the lights of a town, the attractions of shops, picture-houses, and dance halls. You have to give up all idea of being within walking distance of a bus-route. You have to resign yourself to not getting your letters delivered regularly. You have, in fact, to possess a somewhat Wordsworthian cast of mind, and to be one of those of whom that great poet wrote:

> 'The stars of midnight shall be dear
> To her; and she shall lean her ear
> In many a secret place
> Where rivulets dance their wayward round,
> And beauty born of murmuring sound
> Shall pass into her face.'

Does that seem far removed from the Land-girl of today? Not so very far, I think; not necessarily. It depends on the girl. It certainly doesn't apply to those where beauty has only passed on to, not in to, their faces from the beauty-parlour or the little pots on the dressing-table. Wordsworth's beauty was inward, not outward; it was absorbed, not washed off every night. But is it possible, you may ask, that the modern girl, the town girl, should still retain that quality? You may go so far as to agree that Wordsworth's beauty can still be found in the true peasant (I use the word 'peasant' because it is the only word which expresses what I mean, although I know it carries a foreign suggestion in English ears and makes one visualise vineyards and stone-walled terraces between the olives), but you will probably dispute that the average girl of 1944, growing up to such different standards, can find contentment in so ante-dated a mode of existence. Perhaps you think I am making it all up, just in order to throw the most favourable light on the Land Army and its members? If you think that, please read the following letter from a Land-girl, aged twenty-three, and note, please, that she had previously had no less than five years in which to test the allurements of city life.

DOLGOCH,
SOAR-Y-MYNYDD,
TREGARON, CARDIGANSHIRE.
November 10th, 1943

Certainly I can expand upon this wilderness – it happens to be my favourite topic. The difficulty is, where to start? At the moment the kitchen is filled with voluble Welshmen – the three sheep-farmers who came to help this afternoon not having ridden away yet. The kitchen is huge, stone flagged and the men are all toasting themselves round the peat fire – their toes nearly touching the embers as we have a fire flat on the hearth and no fender or civilised nonsense such as hearth-mats. A huge flitch of bacon, one of many, suspended from the ceiling, casts a grotesque shadow over this page and I'm heartily wishing that paraffin were made to burn a little brighter.

We are too high up to come under the ploughing order but a small amount of corn is planted on a patch of ploughed-up hillside for the two working horses and one riding cob we will keep up here through the winter. The corn is very poor stuff – it is all scythed and hand bound, and has considerably more stalk than head, but the animals will be very grateful for it later on.

It is the sheep alone who can pick up a scanty food supply from the mountain grass through the winter – now already bare and brown. On Monday last all the ponies and their suckling foals were rounded up and taken to tack for the winter months down in the lowlands. Many wild with suckling foals – which like the lambs are born out on the hills without human aid at hand – and all with glorious manes and wildly flowing tails. I was sad to see them go

– whenever we climbed up to the peat bogs for rushes or peat loads, we would catch a glimpse of them flying away in the far distance over the plateau-like range tops.

These wild hills extend for miles and are most desolate. Great bogs are found everywhere and craggy ravines with rushing streams and deep pools. A huge lake lies three miles away, once stocked with trout by the monks of the historic old Strata-fleur Abbey. Only an occasional shepherd and the sheep now go near it. Farms four miles away and more are ' neighbours,' all ride over to help each other on the big gathering and shearing days. Almost all have the surname 'Jones,' and most of the Christian names coincide, so all the occupants of a farm take that address for their known surname. Thus I am 'Pat Dalgoch' to all-comers – we have a Davie Nantrwch, Davie Nantmarn, Davie Dalgoch, and a Davie Nantllwyd. (*Nant* is the Welsh word for stream.)

All our water is carried from a spring; a week ago the wireless battery gave out, and it was only yesterday a chance came to take it to be recharged. All news regarding the war was at a stop until then. The horse is the one means of transport up here, all, young and old, ride.

The biggest day of the year is the shearing day in June. Over 120 farmers from far and wide rolled up to shear our 3,000 sheep. All were provided with breakfast, dinner (two courses, cooked), tea and supper. Never have I seen such gigantic supplies of food. Thirty loaves were baked in the old brick oven – and what whoppers they were. The bleating of reluctant lambs, the snipping of the countless shears, laughter and endless Welsh jokes filled the little valley. About sixty ponies were parked on the hill which runs right to the back of the house, and a grand sight they looked.

It is now a year almost since I came here, and it is the constant wonder of the multitude how I manage to 'stick it' as they put it. Before joining the WLA I worked for five long, dreary years in an office in Brixton with 999 other female employees. Circumstance kept my nose to the detested grindstone, though always I dreamt of hills and stars and great free spaces and sometimes, bending over a ledger in springtime – I could actually smell the primroses of my imagination. I was in London all through the blitz, and yet the folk up here have never heard a siren – how strange it seems after that winter of madness.

My mother is Welsh but dad is English, and I was brought up in an English part of Monmouthshire – the district might have been the other side of the equator as far as it compared with this part. Mother taught us no Welsh, but I have now picked up a great deal – it is a very difficult language, however. It still is a disadvantage to a great extent, today, for instance, with the talk rattling along amongst the men. What little I do venture to speak sounds far more expressive than English – our eight sheepdogs (shaggy and faithful) are all Welsh-speaking. Also our five milking cows (household commodities these – we naturally can't sell milk) and, I strongly suspect, our three little 'sweis' or calves, despite their English names – Snowball, Topsy and Punch. These are my endless delight with their huge dreamy eyes and nuzzling noses, which simply won't believe that any bucket has a bottom when I give them the skimmed milk.

Then the broken-in horses – Glasbach, tiny and sturdy; Sam Bach, the swiftest horse for miles despite his 13 years; Ceffyl Du (black horse); Ceffyl Lloyd (white horse) – what an endless joy. All know their way blindfold home through the mountains. Three week ago I rode back from Tregaron at midnight in a pitch-black darkness on the back of Sam. He sped along like an arrow, although I had not the faintest idea where we were. It was quite an experience. I felt as if I was just sitting on his back rushing through the sky at top speed. (I have never ridden before.)

My pen has a dreadful habit of running away with me. The old grandfather clock has ticked out nine o'clock – our neighbours have gone, and the peat fire has, as is its habit, suddenly collapsed.

Thinking over my past year of gay freedom, a thousand things come back to me – winberries as large as plums, huge tufts of heather, peat-cutting in May, the arrival of some forty odd pups at intervals, the river (a baby at this stage) a roaring, flooded monster in September. I love them all, and it is so easy to write of the things one loves, isn't it?

This letter, I find, will be posted tomorrow as there is to

be a funeral in Tregaron. All Welsh funerals are public, so Mr Jones will have to trot off to it. Otherwise you would not have had this until next week, as Simon Jones, the postman, won't be round until Friday again, and is always too late to post that evening in Tregaron.

P.S. – You may be interested to learn that there is a tiny remote chapel in the heart of these hills. Everyone rides there on Sundays and stable their ponies in a specially built stable attached to the church – any religious-minded dogs who follow their masters are shut up there too during the service. A tuning-fork strikes the pitch for hymn singing and often the earnest clerics preach (in Welsh, of course) of the sins of dances, drink, theatres and whist drives. Alas, we have no chance to indulge in such orgies, but many and frequent are the 'Amens' from the scanty, yet suitably impressed shepherd congregation.

The preachers are given weekend hospitality at the farms in turn, and are brought up from Tregaron by pony. Poor timid 'men of God!' most have never ridden before and are by no means lion-hearted as they frantically clutch their steeds by the mane and proceed at less than walking pace.

(*Signed*) Pat Walters

XIX

The WLA in Scotland

The Scottish Land Army is run on very much the same lines as the English, but is a completely separate organisation controlled, not by a Director and headquarters as in England, but by the Department of Agriculture for Scotland. This department, acting for the Secretary of State for Scotland, delegates the duties of local organisations to special Land Army sub-committees set up under the Agricultural Executive Committees for the district; and on each Agricultural Executive Committee a woman member represents the interests of the WLA. There is also a WLA liaison staff, consisting of a chief liaison officer and three area assistants, which maintains a close contact between the Department of Agriculture and the WLA sub-committees.

These slight differences of organisation naturally do not affect the girls in any practical way. Conditions of enrolment, training, employment, hostels, welfare, uniform, maintenance during unemployment, and so on, are much the same in the two countries. Of course local differences, unconnected with organisation, have to be taken into account. For instance, the Scottish farmers, I regret to say, took less kindly than their English colleagues to the idea of employing women, with the result that the growth of the

WLA in the North was comparatively slow. (Employment figures are given in Appendix 4, on page 178) With the increased demand for labour, however, and thanks to the good work of which the girls were proving themselves capable, the prejudice gradually wore down, and we can conclude this paragraph with a little boastful song composed of quotations from various farmers. One, a poultry farmer on a big scale, declared that he never intended to go back to male labour; another, on a mixed farm, wrote to say that if he could get another girl like the one he already had he would sack the horseman he had had to put up with for the past year; another, a large dairy farmer, was so well pleased with his girls that he decided to pay them 4s. a week above their minimum wage. (There never was a greater fallacy than that tiresome old joke about the Scots being mean.) All this, I think, may be taken as practical evidence that the girls have fully proved their worth.

It might be supposed that the different character of the country had determined a great difference also in the nature of farm-employment, but such an idea is probably due to the fact that when we think of Scotland, our imagination rushes instantly to the Highlands with their moors and deer-forests, unproductive from the agricultural point of view though beautiful beyond compare. A glance at the employment table on page 172 will show that the greatest concentration occurs in the dairying counties of the Lowlands – Ayr, Lanark, Fife, Renfrew and Dumbarton, the

Lothians, Dumfries, Roxburgh, Stirling and Clackmannan, Angus, Berwick – and drops with a crash as we travel northwards into Caithness, Sutherland, Nairn, Banff. Naturally, one must take the relative size of the counties into consideration; but after allowing for that it remains evident that the distribution of labour has followed the lines one would expect. Still, it would be rather dull and unromantic if we could discover no particularity at all in the Land-girl's job in that most romantic of countries. She does turn her hand to all the ordinary jobs so familiar to us in England, and especially in the potato-growing areas she makes herself useful – no gardener needs to be reminded of the excellence of Scottish seed-potatoes, and he would be perfectly justified in thinking that at some stage in its life-history, his potato had passed through the hands of a northern Land-girl – but all this is a thing which in the course of the somewhat monotonous recital of the foregoing pages we have come to take for granted. The Scottish girl turns shepherdess, of course, and we may feel that there is something suitable between that traditionally poetic vocation and a mountainous country; visions of the lamb tenderly rescued from a snowdrift, or of the flock called together on a summer's day when the bees are thick among the heather. To judge by some photographs which have appeared in the Press, you might think that what the Scottish shepherdess does with her lambs is to tuck them under her arms and take them for an airing in the streets of

Glasgow, but you would find another story if you read about the girl who left her home at eighteen and four years later was running a 200-acre farm in charge of all the lambing. Shepherding, however, is a job the Scottish girl shares with her sisters in England and Wales, so we must look elsewhere for particularity.

Forestry... True, she shares this also with the English Timber Corps, but there is perhaps something rather special about her mode of life in Scotland, which accords suitably with a wilder land. The English girl finds her lodging in billets, but the Scottish girls usually live in hutted camps in the heart of the woods. This feels like the real thing, a sort of combination of the Red Indian tales of our childhood, the tales of settlers anywhere in the primitive world, and the great lumber-camps we vaguely associate with Canada, huge heaps of sawdust smelling good in the sunny clearing, and enormous logs being shot over the rapids of a river. Perhaps it is not quite so Wild West as all that in Scotland. But there exists, paradoxically, in all of us the desire to get away from the civilisation we have so laboriously created – how else to explain the taste for such uncomfortable pleasures as picnics and caravanning? In these camps the young members of the Scottish Timber Corps can indulge this latent instinct with the maximum of picturesqueness and the minimum of rigour. They run the camps themselves, and, more fortunate than many housewives, can command the services of cooks and orderlies, appointed out of their own number. They are not left entirely to their own devices, of course: their welfare is the responsibility of a Chief Officer with headquarters in Edinburgh, and a staff of seven divisional Welfare Officers who spend their time going round the camps to deal with difficulties and to offer advice.

The girls themselves have first been well conditioned to the heavy work required of them. Most of them were town-girls (it is always the same old story), who knew nothing of the country except what they might have observed on holiday, but I hope it has become clear in the course of those pages that the WLA is a really very sensible organisation, and it was quickly

realised that some preliminary initiation would be necessary. A large country house near Brechin, amongst woods scheduled for felling, was taken and equipped, a male chief instructor appointed, also a number of women instructors, and a regular course instituted. Girls who found they didn't like it were allowed to resign during the first week. Those who stayed on, and they were the majority, were gradually introduced to both theory and practice. The first weeks of the course, they learnt about the technical side of timber production, selection, grading, and so on, also First Aid and Hygiene. A physical-training officer was later added, at a second school opened in Aberdeenshire, and exercises specially designed to develop the necessary muscles were taught; these included axe-swinging, which may have looked funny at the time, but which came in very useful when the swingers had something solid to cut at, not merely the empty air.

Thus apprenticed and prepared, the members of the Timber Corps were found capable of doing all the work normally done by men in the woods-felling, cross-cutting and snedding the trees, drawing them out with either horses or tractors, working the sawmills, loading and stacking pit-props. Any specialist got a specialised rate of pay; and any girl fully replacing a man got a man's full rate. It must not be thought that all of the two thousand girls in the Scottish Timber Corps live in camps; some do live in billets or in requisitioned houses; and some do travel about on acquisition work, as in England and Wales. We have already devoted a great deal of space to a description of this work with its adventures and vicissitudes, but since Scotland is something quite by itself – and how deeply those who love it feel this! We print here another letter as a complementary picture:

'Our job was very far 'behind the men behind the guns.' I believe even our own Headquarters forgot our existence on occasions when we disappeared for weeks at a time into the highlands. The four of us – plus luggage and equipment – packed into a somewhat uncertain car. Setting off from Aberdeen to the north or west and driving to the hilly, tortuous roads where the Dee or the Don splutter into existence on to the broad stretches bordering on the coast.

'No matter what our destination, the weather was rarely kind; a state which did not lend a brighter aspect to the ever important question, 'Where are we going to stay?' The choice was probably between an expensive fishing hotel (which was in any case, on most occasions, too far from the work) or a ' but-and-ben,' often lacking the bare necessities of life. We learnt to prefer the latter. There is nothing so disheartening as to come in from work, cold and wet, to find the bathroom and the fire monopolised by dear old ladies and gentlemen, in the process of taking yet another rest in the country. At least the cottage wife provided what she was able so far as hot water and a bowl was concerned, and however large the family we always managed to squeeze in round the peat-stacked hearth. Brose and oatcakes, too, were far more satisfying than pseudo-English fare with the peculiar Scottish lack of vegetables.

'With the early winter sunset we rarely did any fieldwork on the first day. There were always preparations to make for the survey, pencils to sharpen and compass to check. We would browse over the map and estimate the distance to be climbed before the stand was reached.

'We would be off in the morning (car willing) enveloped in as many clothes as was possible to work in. I was the most unfortunate from the climatic point of view: I had the booking to do. One can imagine that after three hours inactivity half-way up a hillside, a state of rigor mortis is not far off, for the east wind is quite merciless and wet clothes become icy armour. How bad-tempered we would get, and woe-betide her who misread the compass. It is only too easy to lose oneself in a thousand-acre stand and descend several miles from the car, but we were all more or less old hands at our job, and our sense of direction had developed with experience.

'There were days when a bitter calm lay over the countryside and a red sunset made the snow a pink and sparkling carpet. Inquisitive deer considered our species, moving closer, and then streaking off. I felt that without four legs we did not belong there. Man's foolish war had penetrated even this. Nevertheless the beautiful creatures were quite friendly at that season. They would come down the hillside in the evening and accept us as part of the surroundings, which, indeed, we were; particularly after an exciting week when we lived in some stables, cooking over a dilapidated grate and sleeping beneath horse blankets and rubber ground-sheets – covered, I may add, in the blood of many stalked and since-devoured beasts. Porridge was our staple food; the first pot was made at 6.30 a.m., as soon as one noble soul had crept from her chilly couch. The rest of us would follow soon and help to prepare for another day in our small, self-contained community.

'There was never a dull moment for that Acquisition party. We expected little and became adept at providing our own amusement, even though, at times, it sank to the level of sarcasm over our food and the unfortunate cook thereof. Sheila would sit for hours story-telling – she was a Highlander and excelled in making our hair stand on end with her native legends. We heard of her early pole-selecting days when she with three other girls parked their caravan and prepared to work on a 4,000-acre wood, three miles from any house and eight from the nearest village. Snow came and lay in deep drifts which completely cut them off from civilisation. Even the 'postie' failed to get through for a week. Gradually the loneliness and the possibility of food shortage assumed gloomy proportions – evenings seemed longer and longer – and when the supply of lamp oil was exhausted – quite unbearable. The climax came when three of them, sitting one night in the caravan, heard a piercing shriek…'

XX

The WLA in the Isle of Man

The Land Army in the Isle of Man is necessarily small, for the island itself is small, but it exists to the creditable strength of forty-six members. In so restricted an area, it has been found convenient to group these girls into Mobile Squads, operating from the Board of Agriculture's Experimental Farm, two miles from Peel. It is at this farm that the girls receive their training, which consists in practical work as well as lectures on the elements of agriculture. Half the total strength is attached to the Mobile Squads who travel in their own vans driven by one of their number to farms all over the island, in gangs of two, four, six, eight or ten, according to the demands of the farmer, a most practical arrangement suited to so small a place where everywhere is accessible from everywhere else. The other half of the girls are on farms or in market gardens, in the respective proportions of nineteen and four.

They receive the same uniform and replacements as in England, but the wage-rate is a little lower (44s. 6d. a week) and the working hours a little longer (sixty hours a week, with one half day and one Sunday free per fortnight).

XXI

The WLA in Northern Ireland

There is unfortunately very little to say about this, for several most understandable reasons. For one thing, the attractions of the other Women's Services seem to have made a greater appeal to the town-girl who might otherwise have found her way into the Land Army. For another the country-girl, in Northern Ireland, is often the daughter of a farmer and can find her employment ready to hand on her father's farm. Finally, one must remember that compulsory national service has never been introduced in Northern Ireland, and that recruitment for the WLA could therefore never have been expected on a scale comparable to that prevalent in England and Wales, and Scotland.

XXII

Royal Interest

As will be seen from some of the illustrations, their Majesties the King and Queen by their practical interest have offered every encouragement to the WLA. A number of girls are employed on the Sandringham Estate (as also on the Duke of Gloucester's Estate at Barnwell, in Northampton), both on the farm in which His Majesty takes a well-known interest, and also in the woods. In this department they have done every form of work with the exception of felling heavy timber. They have cleaned the ground of weeds and bracken; they have lifted 40,000 young trees for the plantations, and a further 50,000 for the nurseries. They have cut underwood, and tied firewood and faggots; they have taken a course of instruction in pruning and thinning. On the farm they have carried out the usual jobs, sometimes with the assistance of Princess Elizabeth and Princess Margaret Rose, who say the only thing they don't like about the work is having to get up so early.

The Queen could scarcely have given a greater sign of approval than by becoming Patron of the WLA in England, Wales and Scotland, and also of the Benevolent Fund, but this supremely charming lady never does things by halves, and, not content with merely giving her name, proceeded to invite 300 Land-girls to tea with her and the Princesses. Girls were brought to London from all over the country, even from Scotland. ('It is awfully good of you to come all this way,' said the Queen, as she shook hands with them.) None of them had known in advance what they were coming for. This was on the occasion of the fourth birthday of the WLA, in July, 1943, warm summer weather, and the party had first been planned to take place out of doors in the garden at Buckingham Palace. But the Queen, with considerable but characteristic imagination, reversed this decision. Land-girls, she said, saw quite enough of gardens and of out of doors, and she felt sure that the inside of a palace which wasn't quite so much part of their daily life, would interest them far more. So in the great gilded drawing-rooms of the palace the party took place.

XXIII

Courageous Deeds – and Some Stories

'They fight in the fields,'and sometimes they have had to fight in very truth. Not only against weeds and weather, frost and flood; but against fire and angry animals. Bombs and gunfire they have had also, but that has been the common lot, although one would not wish to underestimate for one moment the Land girl's insouciant courage, particularly in the coastal counties of Essex, Norfolk, Suffolk, and the South coast, under air-attack; and even, in East Kent, 'the nearest point to Hitler's Europe,' not under air-attack only but also under shelling from enemy batteries across the Channel. One example may be quoted, which although it received much publicity at the time the triple award was made, must be taken as typical of the experience of many less publicised farms on that exposed shoulder of South-east England. We quote from *The Times* of May 23rd, 1942:

'The King has given orders for the following appointments and awards. For brave conduct in civil defence: George Medal – Gilbert William James Mitchell, farmer. British Empire Medal – Kathleen Mary, Mrs Mitchell, farmer's wife; Miss Grace Lilian Harrison, farm worker (now tractor driver, Women's Land Army).

'Mr And Mrs Mitchell and Miss Harrison have made an unexampled effort and shown sustained bravery and devotion to duty in carrying on farming under the gunfire and air attacks of the enemy. The farm is at the nearest point to the Continent and is scarred with filled-in shell-holes. The farm buildings are probably the most vulnerable in the country, yet work was carried on throughout the Battle of Britain and ever since. During intense air raids the German pilots machine-gunned the farm and work on the land had to be stopped, but in spite of all the difficulties and dangers there was no change in the routine of milking and attending to the stock. When cutting corn, Mr Mitchell and Miss Harrison often had to take cover under the tractor or binder when German pilots were machine-gunning. On one occasion, when Mr Mitchell was driving the tractor, a balloon nearby was shot down in flames. The burning fabric fell across the tractor but was quickly extinguished by Mr Mitchell, who then carried on with his work. Mr And Mrs Mitchell, with the help of Miss Harrison, remained at the farm and not only saved their own crops, but also those of other farms which had been evacuated.'

Miss Harrison and the Mitchells, lavishly interviewed by the Press, added a few details to this account. Yes, it was true that during machine-gunning they had sometimes dived under the tractor. Yes, it was true that the farm was scarred with shell holes: on some days as many as two hundred shells had fallen. In spite of that, they said, a couple of sheep had been the only casualties; and although a bomb had fallen in the midst of the cows, by some miracle not one had been injured. Yes, it was true that the three of them, with one faithful old shepherd, had carried on through the Battle of Britain after all the other farmhands had left. Yes, Grace Harrison was only seventeen then. Yes, there were 120 acres on the farm, quite enough for four people to take on and help their neighbours as well. 'But the war is only a sideshow after all. The real show is the farm.'

A superb phrase, that. It holds all the contemptuous arrogance of the British, and all the monosyllabic Churchillian simplicity and swank as well. Who can say that we have lost the gift which informed the Elizabethan makers of our language? Or the spirit which kept England going when the Armada appeared on that same Channel? One wishes that phrase could be brought to the notice of Hitler, who thought he could starve Britain. His war a sideshow... *Some* sideshow, he might reply. Yes, but the farm is the thing. Britain's farms will feed the people of Britain. And so they have, up to seventy-five per cent, two-thirds of the total production needed. They fight in the fields...

There was another Land-girl, an ex-librarian, a peaceable occupation, if ever there was one. On the lonely farm where she worked near Dover, she came under much shelling and bombing, and was personally singled out for attention in machine-gunning three times by a diving plane. The War Agricultural Committee's badge for courage is now hers.

Near Portsmouth, some girls were supplied with tin hats, and wrote back saying that they were very grateful but wished their cows could have tin hats as well, since shrapnel sometimes fell plentifully when they were getting the herd in at 5 a.m.

After a raid on Canterbury, ten out of eleven Land-girls from a bombed house reported for work next morning at the usual time. The eleventh apologised for being late, but explained that she had had to be dug out of the debris.

During another night raid on Canterbury, another girl bicycled through the burning streets to the farm where she worked, because she was worried about the cows. Having satisfied herself that they were unhurt, she bicycled back through the city to have a look at some horses in which she was interested. Then, as night was growing into morning, she returned to milk the cows. She was awarded the County Badge for Courage, but was quite surprised when the Press descended on her. 'It was my job to look after the cows,' she said, 'and as for going back to milk them, the milk was wanted and the cows needed milking, and that was all there was to it.'

Quite simple, isn't it?

These stories do not exhaust the list, and one could add many stories about airmen dragged by Land-girls from crashed planes, ricks set on fire by incendiary bombs, oil-drums carried out from burning barns – and even a story about a blazing railway truck which was got under control with the help of six members of the Timber Corps who happened to be at hand, barelegged and their hair still prettily decorated with wild-flowers picked during their luncheon-hour.

But these are either war-stories, or else incidents that might happen to anybody at any time. The speciality of the agricultural worker, and consequently of his handmaid the Land girl, is what happens on the farm owing to the unreasonable behaviour of their dumb beast friends. Bulls…Quite a lot of people will carefully skirt round a field which contains mere cows, under the comforting reflection that they could dive through the hedge should somebody's Buttercup or Daisy come at a cumbrous trot towards them; but bulls!… One doesn't readily go near bulls. And how right they are in this conviction. The bull is a creature of incalculable impulses, apt to turn even against those who have brought him up from the bucket. He runs at his farmer-owner, who is flung to the ground, rendered unconscious, gored, and saved only by the intervention of a Land-girl, herself injured, but staggering again to her feet. He runs amok in the night, and again the Land-girl, armed with a pitchfork, rescues her employer who has already been thrown five times up and down. He pins a farm-hand against the loose-box wall, and the Land-girl comes up, kicks the bull to divert his attention, and drags the farm-hand out to

safety. He fights with another bull in the field – surely rather bad management on the part of the farmer to put them in there together – and again the Land-girl comes up to help her employer in separating them. He attacks sheep, tossing a ewe in the air, and would toss the twin lambs also, but for the counter attack of the Land-girl who drops the chicken-feed she is carrying, dashes through four strands of barbed wire, yells, kicks the bull with the toe of her boot, and grabs the lambs up under either arm. 'I don't know whether the bull was startled by the yell or the kick,' said the farmer, 'but it tossed its tail in the air and went off down the field as though stung by a gadfly.'

One girl, who had been dragged round the farmyard, and twice thrown to the ground under the bull's feet, but who held on all the same, remarked afterwards that she liked this life, it was so much more interesting than office work. She looked quite puzzled when somebody said there was no accounting for tastes.

Passing from war-stories and danger-stories to oddments of individual experience, one again finds that the Land-girl has not always had a dull or monotonous time. Amongst the thousands who have just plodded on, doggedly and usefully, there have been some who more startlingly stand out – as must always happen in any company of people. Life rewards the enterprising. There comes, for instance, a story from Hampshire of a farmer taken away to hospital, leaving no one but his two Land-girls to run his 150-acre farm, his dairy-herd of twenty cows, his thirty-five ewes about to lamb, and not a man on the place to give a hand. For five weeks those girls worked from 5.30 every morning (in mid-winter too), never took a day off, never lost a lamb or a calf.

Another girl and her sister in Devon ran a farm for the

owner who was away in the Forces. These girls had never worked for their living before, but they took up their very primitive quarters in the top storey of one of the outbuildings, declared that they were completely happy, vowed that they never wished to return to an idle life, and gaily took charge of a large herd of pedigree pigs, a few cows, a great many poultry, three horses, and seventy acres of land. Not content with this, they had helped to make a road, to put up a new Dutch barn, and to clear a spinney of trees and scrub in order to gain a few more acres of arable land.

More than one girl has bought a cow of her own, which she looks after in her spare time. What a difference between those who complain that they haven't any spare time and those who can always make it! One of these girls that I have in mind, lives at home, works on a local farm, and keeps her two cows in her home paddock; another one has induced her employer to let her cow run with his own herd.

There are girls too, who, wanting to do something out of the ordinary, have taken up the study of scientific soil-testing. I like also the story of the two girls who were so much upset by the death of their horse that they carried out a secret autopsy on the huge carcase to discover what had been wrong. Zest could scarcely go further.

An odd little story comes from Flintshire. Here, a gang of nine girls was working on a piece of land which was constantly getting flooded by a hidden spring. It was then discovered that one of the girls possessed a peculiar gift of water-divining with a hazel rod.

Is it perhaps a little frivolous to mention romance in connection with the solid achievements of the WLA? But romance has not been lacking. Sometimes it has even been mixed in with the solid achievement, as in the case of one girl who got married in the morning and was out harvesting again in the afternoon, having made her bridegroom and the wedding guests come to help.

Another girl wrote to ask for leave as she was getting married the same day as her husband.

XXIV
The Future of the Land-girl

We have left to the very end the most important question of all: What will become of the Land-girl after the war is over? It is the most important, because after all the war, in the sense of actual fighting, is temporary: even in our gloomiest moments we do know one thing for certain, and that is that it must come to an end some day. That is as sure as death itself. And what then?

Naturally, this is not a question which affects only the Land-girl among the myriads of young women who have taken to some most unexpected mode of life during these temporary years. It is a question so enormous, and so deeply involved with so many other things, that it is impracticable to discuss it here in a whittled-down way without the consciousness of omitting too many considerations, too many qualifying parentheses. It is impossible to take anything like a comprehensive view. So our only chance is to discuss the specific problem of the future for the girl who has worked on the land, and not the general future of emancipated young womanhood.

Roughly speaking, the Land-girls may be grouped under five headings:-

(1) Those who wish to return to their former occupations, or to something similar.

(2) Those who had no former occupation.

(3) Those who wish to 'go abroad.'

(4) Those who will marry.

(5) Those who wish to remain on the land.

We will take these five groupings in order.

(1) Those who wish to return to their former occupations will find either that their former job is again open for them (and this is where the efficient and valuable girl will score, the girl whose employer has missed her and is anxious to have her back), or else they will have to face the normal competitive scramble for seats. Here, the Benevolent Fund can help with refresher courses for a girl who has lost something of her old skill.

(2) The case of those who had no former occupation is different. Many a girl will find herself technically untrained and unequipped for any other profession or career, when the moment comes for the Land Army to be honourably dissolved. In some ways she will, of course, have gained some valuable experience during her years of service on the land. She will have learnt the need for punctuality, and for the give-and-take involved always when you are working with other people. She will have acquired all sorts of odd bits of knowledge about life in general and human nature in particular. She will almost certainly have derived considerable benefit to

her physical health. But in spite of this all-round gain on the swings she may have sacrificed something on the roundabouts. This lack of technical proficiency will be owing to no fault of hers, and indeed in many cases will be due only to that most laudable impulse which sent her into the WLA 'because I wanted to do something for my country' before her calling-up age-group had been reached. Seventeen, it must be remembered, is the age at which a girl may enter the WLA, that is, younger than the age for compulsory national service. She could thus have devoted the intervening time to her own advantage. But she didn't, and as a result she will find herself left at the end of the war with little proficiency except perhaps in dung-spreading or in cutting down enormous trees.

Now it seems quite likely that she may not wish to continue doing this all her life, and that she may prefer to devote herself to one of the many other careers now available to women. It is most interesting to speculate on the careers which may be open to them after the war. Quite apart from the agricultural jobs – and we may hope that agriculture is in future going to be a prosperous industry with the country population receiving some consideration from the Government – there are likely to be many openings for women which hitherto have scarcely existed at all. For example: milk-recorders, vets, and assistant vets; assistants in laboratory and research work. Then there will also be a demand for teachers in rural domestic economy and other instructional jobs. For years country people have been urging that teachers in country schools should have some knowledge of country life. The Board of Education is now working out schemes to meet the increased need for teachers under the new Education Bill; members of the WLA will be able to apply for training as teachers, with full confidence that the Board is alive to the value of their experience already acquired on the land.

Fortunately, the case of the girl who feels the need for some training is a case in which both the Land Army and the Government can do something constructive. There is the Land Army Benevolent Fund itself, and the Government training scheme. The resources available to the Fund for this purpose after the war will naturally depend on the amount of money raised and also on how much will remain after meeting the demands for benefits during the war years. It is hoped that there will be enough to help those girls who wish to take up a new occupation. Government plans for post-war training are at present still some what indefinite, but they are in the process of being worked out, and the Land Army should be able to share in whatever schemes may be made available to the members of the other services.

Girls who are beginning to wonder what to do with

themselves after the war are advised to look at the table on page 184, where they will find a list of possible careers and also an address where they can obtain further information.

(3) Those who wish to 'go abroad.' The majority of these, presumably, are those who wish to continue in agriculture, but some confusion seems sometimes to exist in their minds as to what they mean by 'abroad.' Do they mean liberated Europe, or do they mean our own colonies and Dominions? They don't always seem to know. If they mean the former, then it would be a more or less temporary solution of their future, a 'reconstruction' idea, which must come to an end in time when some sort of resettlement is arrived at, and the deported peasant population of Europe has been safely restored to their original homes. (I should like to see the look on the face of a French or Belgian farmer when he arrives back on his holding after years of enforced labour in a German war-factory, and finds his fields taken in charge by a couple of British Land-girls. Perhaps he would keep them on – who knows?)

If they mean the latter, i.e., our own colonies or Dominions, then they are talking about something far more permanent. When the Land Army was disbanded after the last war, many members took advantage of the free passage to the Dominions offered to ex-service women. It is much to be hoped that the same thing may happen again. It seems likely that it will, for young women today are far more enterprising and adventurous than they were even in 1919, and what could be more desirable than that the stock of these fine girls should mix with their consanguineous friends in Canada, Australia, New Zealand?... I can visualise a new 'Mayflower,' blossoming on every deck with the waving hands of a new sort of pioneer, a sort which would have astonished our Mayflower forefathers whose women were encumbered by huge skirts and tight stomachers, and encumbered even more by the convenient prejudices established by man for the control of his subservient woman. My new Mayflower carries a different muster. It carries gay young creatures, untrammelled by bulky clothes; legs are allowed to appear as legs, breeched and gaitered; the soft loose jersey replaces the whale-boned bodice, the elastic belt replaces the rigidity of the unnatural corset. And above all the liberty of the spirit replaces the rigidity of the conventional mind.*

By the way, a strange idea appears to exist among Land-girls, to the effect that they may be *compelled* to 'go abroad' after the war. Let me contradict this

---

* Information can be obtained from the Society for the Oversea Settlement of British Women 3, Sanctuary Buildings, Great Smith Street, London, SWI.

idea emphatically and at once. Land Army officials are much puzzled to know how it can have got about. If a girl wants to go either into liberated Europe or into the colonies or Dominions, it will be entirely by her own choice. The idea of compulsion is without any foundation whatsoever, it just waves vaguely about in the air, and has roots only in the minds of those who like to believe in any stray bit of gossip they may have heard or may perhaps have read in some irresponsible newspaper.

(4) Those who will marry. What can we say to these, beyond wishing them happiness, almost the best thing one can wish to any human being? Many Land-girls already wear an engagement ring on the third finger of their left hand. It usually represents some boy in the Air Force or the fighting Services. Sometimes it represents a farmer or a man on the farm. Whichever it is, may they find happiness together.

(5) Those who wish to remain on the land come last on our list, but are those who require our most important consideration. They are those who will demand the most constructive effort on the part of the WLA and the Ministry of Agriculture in particular, and of the Government in general. Some provision will have to be made for these girls who have decided that they prefer country life; who do not wish to return to the stifling enclosure of shops and offices; who have breathed the

open air now for so many years; who have become hardened to the austerities and no longer count them as such, but accept them, rather, as the necessary price to pay for the return of freedom, interest, and attendant pleasure. 'Oo, I wouldn't like to go back to selling underwear... Oo, I wouldn't like to go back to that roomful of clacking typewriters... Oo, I don't want to go back to all those rows of figures... Oo, I don't want to be shut in any more...' She actually shudders as she says it, like a prisoner faced with going back to a cell.

Shut in. Shut in. There are people who really feel like that. Many people who accepted the shut-in life because it had never occurred to them to do anything else, or who had vaguely felt that they liked the country, and then did nothing about it because their steps seemed set into the urban way. The majority of people are slow to get out of the way that has been ordered for them by their usual life and by their antecedents. It takes either great personal energy and enterprise, or else the upheaval of war, to open your eyes to what you really want to do.

For some Land-girls this enforced opportunity has come as a real eye-opener. They have found themselves; and to find yourself is to discover your true vocation.

Now the Land-girl who wishes to remain on the land is in a completely different position from her sisters who have gone into the ATS, the WAAF, or the WRNS, the

WVS or the NFS. They may have scored heavily over her during the war: they have worn a smarter uniform; they have had the advantage of belonging to a more corporate and more showy body; they have never been called Cinderellas, they have had their fun and also their dramatic showiness while it lasted. But their show will be over once the war is over. The need for their service will automatically come to an end. This is where the Land-girl, poor Cinderella, will at last score. Her war-time job is not a temporary but a perennial job. Her concern has not been with endangered convoys, with air-attacks, with radio-location, with blazing streets; it has been with the steady, level, unchanging business of agriculture, a business which has gone on ever since man first learnt that he could draw milk from his cow and could beat flour from his wheat. She is the inheritor of this long tradition. All other things which women have done during this war, however courageous, however competent, must necessarily seem temporary when measured against the backward and forward stretching of the obligation of husbandry. War will cease; but farming will go on.

The Land-girl, however, will be faced with one major difficulty: the return of the men to the farms. It would be a mere waste of time to pretend that a woman can do the heavy work as well as a man; her physical strength precludes it. Agriculture is, in fact, one of those professions in which a man is fully justified in receiving the high wage: he gives better value for his time and money. I think most farmers would agree that the ratio would work out at three women equalling two men, so obviously the man's higher wage-rate cancels out, i.e., three women at 48s. a week comes to 144s. a week, two men at 65s. a week comes to 130s. a week; and, moreover, you have fewer people for whom accommodation has to be provided. It thus seems extremely unlikely that women will oust men to any great extent on the farms, and indeed no reasonable person would wish them to do so.

But there still remain the lighter tasks associated with husbandry, in which physical toughness counts for less. We have already suggested that women appear to be peculiarly well suited to all branches of horticulture, which can be extended to the nursery work in forestry (re-afforestation will be an urgent need after the devastation consequent upon the war), and there are other ploys about the farm where a woman is 'quite as good' as a man. Milking, dairy-work, poultry, shepherding, and the care of young stock come instantly to mind. Pruning and fruit-picking too – though in the fruit-growing counties the picking is usually done by the local women as seasonal labour.

It is hoped that the Benevolent Fund will be able to provide for scholarships, bursaries, loans, grants, etc., to

enable Land-girls to take a course at an agricultural or horticultural training centre in order to improve their qualifications, with a view either to taking up a paid job or to starting on their own.

That, then, is more or less the outlook for the girl who wants to stay on the land. We must confess that it is limited and not so bright as we could wish. But my own idea – which is entirely personal and backed by no official approval at all, in fact I have never put it forward to anyone but have merely let it simmer in my own mind – is that some kind of small-holding scheme (possibly on the Land Settlement Estates) could be devised to meet the desires and ambitions of a certain number of picked girls. This is where the 'starting on their own' comes in. It might not absorb many, only a few hundreds perhaps, out of the few thousands who will be anxious to continue in agriculture; but at least those few hundred would find fulfilment; they would have no sense of being thwarted or frustrated in life, and to have a little nut or kernel of contented people is surely of some value not only to themselves but to the community.

These small-holdings that I envisage would naturally be manned by the cream of the Land Army; by girls, that is, who had in some way managed to come to the top; girls who had earned their proficiency badges, girls who had taken the forewoman's course, or who had specialised in some branch or other. It is unlikely that any but this type of girl would care to take on so much responsibility and management. The holdings would have to be provided, equipped and stocked by government subsidy, since few Land-girls are in possession of any capital of their own; they would, in fact, become small model farms, which should show a reasonable return of interest on the capital outlay and should also at any rate cover the running expenses. I do not imagine that any profit would be obtained, or even expected, for a number of years. But is the scheme Utopian? It is true that it would at first operate on a very tiny scale, but, if it proved a success, might lead to expansion, and in course of time might absorb quite a number of country-minded girls as trainees under the direction of their more experienced sisters.

The whole point, of course, is that the holdings should really be a model. I am not suggesting that a group of girls should take over the management of a mixed farm and run it in the ordinary way. I am suggesting that these Government-controlled holdings should be something of an innovation; something which gave scope for work of an experimental type. The war has taught farmers that it is possible to depart from the rather lazy old methods, and to obtain results from doing things which must have outraged their fathers in their graves. There seems no good reason to suppose that we have come to an end of experimental possibilities, or that there are not many lessons we might profitably learn from other countries. Denmark, for instance, has surely much to teach us... And, to take but one minor example, to do with horticulture rather than agriculture, look at the cloche-system of market-gardening so long practised in France and in the Channel Islands, but almost entirely ignored here until necessity forced its advantages upon the attention of vegetable-growers. I can quite well imagine one of my ideal little holdings entirely sparkling as the sun strikes on rows and regiments of miniature glass barns sheltering the jade-green lettuce for the early market.

Suggestions occur in flocks to the mind. I see mushroom sheds and pedigree poultry runs; I see acres of flowering bulbs. Before the war a prosperous bulb-growing industry had been started in England, notably in Lincolnshire, and although no one would wish to injure the centuries-old industry of those sturdy allies the Dutch, to whose bulb-farms the war has brought such horrible damage already, there still seems room for a little healthy competition in England. Especially now that owing to the wise export policy of the Board of Trade we have begun to build up a market in America.

However, such tentative suggestions must wait until such time as the Government have given due consideration to the problem in general, and in particular to the possible settlement of ex-service men and women on the land. Even so, there will still remain the larger number who will wish to carry on in the usual way on the farm, in the forest, or in the garden, and it is only their due that the Land Army should remember their interest when the time comes.

Obviously, if the girl is to be helped, she must also be prepared to help herself, a little moral which has been pointed out two or three times already in the foregoing pages, but we seem now to have arrived at the point where some practical suggestions might be given. It is not much good saying 'Be bright! Be enterprising! Make yourself indispensable!' without adding some indication of how the necessary qualifications are to be acquired. You can be as bright and enterprising as Nature has made you, thus giving you a good start, but you want to back it up by some technical knowledge.

The Ministry of Agriculture and the organisation of the WLA wisely made it possible for any Land-girl to acquire such knowledge should she desire to do so. The Forewoman's Course has already been alluded to, but two further opportunities were also on offer. One is the Proficiency Tests Course, which carries with it a badge and certificate for the successful candidate. An abbreviated synopsis of this Course is given on page 179. The other, a Correspondence Course in Agriculture and Horticulture, lasted from November 1934, to March 1944, and consisted of nine papers on the Elements of Agriculture arranged by the College of Estate Management, at a charge of 15s. to the student; and of twelve papers on each subject arranged by the Royal Horticultural Society at a charge of £1 for each subject chosen, the subjects being Vegetable Production, Fruit Production, Crops under Glass. The papers were sent out at intervals of a fortnight; the students were required to answer certain questions in writing; these exercises were then read and corrected by a tutor, and returned to the student with corrections or comments.

The Agricultural Course was supplemented by a

text-book, *The Farmer's Year* by J. A. Scott-Watson. An abbreviated synopsis of this course is given on page 181.

If readers will take the trouble to turn up the references to these two courses on pages 181 and 182, and respectively, I feel sure that they will be much impressed (*a*) by the opportunities offered to the willing Land-girl, and (*b*) by the amount she can learn and ought to learn, if she wants to. No Land-girl, and I am thinking especially of those who want to remain on the land after the war is over, has any right to complain that she hasn't been given the chance to equip herself with an enlarged knowledge, and, in fact, the keenness shown by volunteers to take advantage of the opportunities has been most heartening. In 1943, for instance, 1,275 took the Agriculture Correspondence Course, and 630 the Horticultural Course.

We have already referred to the table of possible careers given on page 184, and may here mention that among the jobs listed are some of especial interest to Land-girls: horticulture, agriculture, dairying, market-gardening; and, of course, emigration (types of emigrants required by the Dominions), but apart from these there are forty-nine other careers suggested, provisionally are ranged, under the headings of Women in Industry, Offices and Shops, Domestic Economy, Work with Young Children, Public Health, Professions and Social Services. The variety is encouraging, and ranges from Scientific work (which might mean anything) to Kindergarten teaching.

Appendix I

Women's Land Army Employment Figures

COUNTY	*End Dec. 1939*	*End Dec. 1940*	*End Dec. 1941*	*End Dec. 1942*	*End July 1943*	*End Dec. 1943*
Bedfordshire	24	55	140	492	792	990
Berkshire	103	214	534	1,047	1,291	1,209
Buckinghamshire	54	108	403	1,346	1,778	1,836
Huntingdonshire, Cambridgeshire and Ely	63	113	428	828	1,276	1,307
Cheshire	100	259	570	1,205	1,566	1,426
Cornwall	41	105	292	831	1,311	1,411
Cumberland and Westmoreland	29	119	282	775	1,071	974
Derbyshire	30	78	158	331	505	533
Devonshire	114	164	391	1,047	1,665	1,708
Dorsetshire	103	—	319	712	867	881
Durham	5	—	156	568	1,030	1,008
Essex	124	160	795	2,509	3,751	3,777
Gloucestershire	156	301	537	1,125	1,406	1,344
Hampshire	138	421	866	1,801	2,115	2,248
Isle of Wight	62	—	173	290	428	363
Herefordshire	47	88	255	509	601	650
Hertfordshire	65	138	445	1,623	2,288	2,162
Kent	262	475	1,691	3,126	4,169	3,984
Lancashire	81	185	540	1,174	1,478	1,457
Leicestershire and Rutland	120	172	627	1,704	2,274	2,145
Holland	16 ⎫	126	—	1,308	⎰ 588	536
Kesteven	126 ⎭				⎱ 1,002	918
Lindsey	217	118	291	586	814	740
London and Middlesex	17	—	131	367	581	600
Monmouthshire	34	91	266	499	634	648
Norfolk	112	166	481	1,087	1,446	1,620
Northamptonshire	93	165	543	1,481	1,800	1,834

COUNTY	End Dec. 1939	End Dec. 1940	End Dec. 1941	End Dec. 1942	End July 1943	End Dec. 1943
Northumberland	180	122	373	976	1,276	1,386
Nottinghamshire	29	104	452	1,023	1,261	1,299
Oxfordshire	115	193	410	816	1,053	1,090
Shropshire	103	155	372	861	1,035	1,002
Somersetshire	163	238	454	1,298	1,793	1,794
Staffordshire	65	131	268	676	847	777
Suffolk (East)	90	74	217	758	1,114	1,138
Suffolk (West)	222	230	214	523	646	594
Surrey	121	271	781	1,506	2,329	2,361
Sussex (East)	153	239	771	1,676	2,298	2,022
Sussex (West)	226	222	489	1,229	1,563	1,564
Warwickshire	103	187	412	1,351	1,814	1,762
Wiltshire	162	308	593	1,113	1,538	1,535
Worcestershire	102	224	561	1,392	1,857	1,800
Yorkshire (East)	23	—	—	—	1,124	1,091
Yorkshire (North and West)	89	219	1,075	3,776	4,405	4,088
North Wales	40	—	228	577	541	553
South Wales	30	150	294	628	420	360
Breconshire and Radnorshire	—	—	101	283	326	304
Denbighshire	53	67	136	—	505	575
Flintshire	10	67	104	359	512	602
Glamorganshire	49	—	—	—	764	698
Montgomeryshire	12	—	—	—	243	211
Pembrokeshire	8	—	—	—	447	406

General employment analysis, December 1943:–

    In private employment:

(a) Milkers, ~~or milking and general farm work~~	20,159
(b) In other farm employment, not including milking	12,521
(c) Horticultural employment	10,817
(d) In other jobs	26,374
Employed by War Agricultural Executive Committees	28,374
Timber Corps	4,339

Appendix II
Local Representative's Report

County .... Date of visit .... 194 ....

1. Name of Volunteer .... WLA No ....

2. Billet Address ....

3. Name of employer ....

4. Is employer satisfied? .... 5. Is volunteer satisfied? ....

6. Are billets satisfactory? ....

7. Is volunteer on local doctor's panel? ....

8. Is volunteer member of an approved society? ....

9. Are wages and overtime correctly paid? ....

10. If overtime is worked regularly, what are the average hours in the working week?............

11. How much time off is given each week?.........................

12. What arrangements are made for other leave? ....

13. Does volunteer take/see the Land-Girl? ....
    (If subscription due, please collect and forward to county office)

14. What arrangements have been made for recreation? ....

15. General Remarks:-

....
Signature

Note – Comments on uniform should not be made on this form.

Appendix III
Relative Work-outputs of Women

According to the report prepared by J. H. Smith, M.Sc., Dept. of Agricultural Economics, University College of Wales, Aberystwyth

(Output of adult male = 100)

	Relative work output		Relative work output

TENDING LIVESTOCK:

Poultry 101

Milking 91

Cattle 72

FIELD WORK WITH HORSES:

Driving hay mower 80

Horse raking 71

Rolling 71

Carting 69

Harrowing 68

Ploughing 65

Odd jobs 62

TRACTOR WORK:

Driving, excluding repairs . 73

Driving and repairs 49

POTATO CROP:

Planting (setting) 95

Lifting (picking) 91

Weeding 75

Riddling and sorting . . . 85

Sacking 61

Loading 44

OTHER ROOT CROPS:

Hoeing beet and turnips . 77

Lifting swedes and turnips 70

Lifting mangolds 68

MARKET GARDENING:

Planting brassicas 90

Cutting cabbage 83

	Relative work output		*Relative work output*

LOADING AND SPREADING DUNG:

Loading. 46

Spreading 58

HOEING AND WEEDING:

Hoeing: general. 88

Weeding: general 88

corn (miscell.). . . 79

wheat 84

barley 84

HARVEST OPERATIONS:

Turning hay 92

Self-binding 51

Stooking 63

Loading sheaves 61

Rick work: hay 67

corn 64

Threshing: general . . . 70

cutting bands . . . 91

Bagging and netting

cabbage 81

Pulling peas 103

Pulling broad beans . . . 96

Pulling runner beans . . 101

COMMERCIAL HORTICULTURE:

Cutting flowers. 106

Bunching flowers. . . . 106

Packing flowers. 101

FRUIT PICKING:

Plums. 99

Apples 95

Cherries 95

Small fruit 100

NOTE – It should be understood that these percentages apply to the typical women in agriculture and not only to members of the WLA.

Appendix IV

Scottish Women's Land Army

County	Total	County	Total
Aberdeen	615	Midlothian	545
Angus	241	Moray	111
Argyll	162	Nairn	60
Ayr	1,160	Orkney	6
Banff	95	Peebles	104
Berwick	322	Perth	363
Bute	60	Renfrew (*see under* Dunbarton)	
Caithness	29	Ross and Cromarty	188
Clackmannan (*see under* Stirling)		Roxburgh	333
Dumfries	330	Selkirk	56
Dunbarton and Renfrew	449	Stirling and Clackmannan	269
East Lothian	390	Sutherland	21
Fife and Kinross	664	West Lothian	117
Inverness	139	Wigtown	210
Kincardine	113	Zetland	7
Kinross (*see under* Fife)			
Kirkcudbright	235		
Lanark	582		

Appendix V
WLA Proficiency Tests

Examinations both practical and oral were held in the following branches of land work:-

> Milking and dairy work.
> General farm work.
> Poultry.
> Tractor driving.
> Outside garden and glasshouse work.
> Fruit work.
> Pest destruction.

As a sample of the details required from candidates, we give milking and dairy work:

PRACTICAL: HAND MILKING

Marks awarded for the following points:

Personal cleanliness and suitability of dress.

Management and grooming of cow. (Quick and thorough cleaning of udder, method of approach.)

Skill in milking. (Dry hand milking, general style, grip and motion.)

Efficient stripping.

Sediment test.

Time taken by competitor.

ORAL

Feeding and management (to include health and ill-health) calving; infectious diseases; precautionary measures against mastitis.

Calf-rearing (to include feeding and ailments).

Dairy-work (to include milk-cooling; sterilising of utensils; reasons for producing clean milk).

Appendix VI
Correspondence Course: Agriculture

1. The plant. (The seed and seedling; the root; the stem; the leaf; the flower. Conditions necessary for healthy plant growth.)

2. The soil. (Soil types; temperatures; organisms; fertility; manuring, whether with organic manures or fertilisers.)

3. Grassland. (Herbage plants, grasses, clovers, etc.; growth of herbage; management of pasture and meadows; haymaking.)

4. Tillage. (Implements; weed control; classification of crops; rotation of crops; pests and diseases of crops.)

5. Arable crops. (Root crops; forage crops; flax; pulse crops; clover, sainfoin, lucerne; 'seeds' or one-year leys; temporary leys; ensilage.)

6. The animal. (Its body, digestion, etc.; feeding and feeding stuffs.)

7. Dairy farming. (The dairy-cow; herds; the herd; feeding for milk; housing; milking; milk composition and milk products.)

8. Calf-rearing; animal health and diseases; beef cattle; sheep, pigs, poultry.

9. The farm horse. (Breeding; general management; feeding; grooming; care of feet and legs.) Tractors. (Types of tractor; care of tractor.) Care of farm machinery.

Appendix VII
A Typical Forewoman's Course

SYNOPSIS OF LECTURES

Lecture on Agriculture.
Lecture on the Cow, comprising:

> Breeds of Cattle and their uses.

> Value of milk recording. Principles of breeding.

General management of cows and calf-rearing.
Demonstrations on farm machinery.
Whole days on drainage and cleaning of land, comprising visits to gangs at work.
Lectures on First Aid.

> Income Tax.

> Time Sheets, Sick Pay and Workmen's Compensation.

> War Agricultural Committee Organisation.

> Management of Farms, and labour and duties of Forewomen.

> Leisure and Recreation.

> Social Hygiene (VD).

> Leadership.

> Duties of Forewomen in Hostels.

Visits to a farm and a market garden accompanied in each case by the owner, who explains system or cropping and stocking.

PRACTICAL OPERATIONS
(Under a full-time ex-bailiff instructor)

Hoeing and singling mangolds, and setting gang to work.
Shocking and tying sheaves, and setting gang to work.
Haymaking and rick building and thatching.
Cleaning with bagging hooks.
Using handbill and slasher on hedges and laying a hedge.
Using pick and shovel and laying drain pipes.
Digging a post-hole, and fencing.
Using a brake; grooming and harnessing horse.
Wet day jobs of sawing wood with various saws; making
   thatching pegs.
Sharpening tools and care of tools.

MACHINERY

Seen at work and explained:

Tractor.
Reaper and binder.
Plough and adjustments.
Mower – sharpening knives
   with special file.
Cultivator.
Disc harrow and points.
Gang rollers.
Hay rake.

Horse shimmer.
Acid spray.
Oiling and greasing and
care of machinery;
   sharpening and cleaning
   tools.
Notes given on manure
   drill.

Appendix VIII

Suggested Post-war Careers for Women

Address for information: The Advisory Department, The Women's Employment Federation, 7, Cromwell Place, London, SW7. Who will be pleased to answer enquiries. A very small fee is charged, but this can be waived in cases of real need.

PROFESSIONS AND SOCIAL SERVICES, Etc.

Outdoor Jobs:
> Horticulture.
> Agriculture.
> Poultry.
> Dairying.
> Market Gardening.

Emigration:
> Type of emigrants required by Dominions.

Professions:
> Teaching.
> Law.
> Accountancy.
> Architecture.
> Librarianship.
> Scientific Work.

SOCIAL SERVICES:
  House Property Management.
  Probation Officer.
  Family Case Work (SSAFA).
  Youth Work (Clubs, etc.).
  Policewomen. Church Work.
  Moral Welfare.

PUBLIC HEALTH

Medicine.
Dentistry.
Nursing (specialisation, orthopaedic, tubercular, etc.).
Radiography.
Massage.
Occupational Therapy.
Speech Therapy.
Health Visiting.
Maternity and Infant Welfare.
Midwifery.
Pharmacy, Dispensing.
Hospital Almoning.

WORK WITH YOUNG CHILDREN

Nursery Nurses.
Nursery School Work, Crèches.
Teaching: Kindergarten, Froebel.
Child Guidance Work.

DOMESTIC ECONOMY

Canteen (Factory, etc.).

Cooking and Catering (British Restaurants).

Institutional Management.

Dietetics.

Invalid Cookery (especially for children – St. Thomas's).

Domestic Service and Home Helps (probable future status and reorganisation of service).

WOMEN IN INDUSTRY

Floor Supervisors.

Storekeepers.

Draughtswomen.

Engineering (probable glut).

Time and Motion Study.

Women's Electrical Association.

OFFICES AND SHOPS

OFFICES:

Clerical (Shorthand Typists, Filing, Book-keeping).

Foreign Correspondents.

Civil Service.

SHOPS:

Saleswomen.

Designers and Cutters.

Fine Needlework .

Hairdressing and Beauty Culture.

Commercial Travelling.

Appendix IX
Miscellaneous Items of Information

Uniform
On joining the WLA every girl is supplied with the following:
2 green jerseys, 2 pairs of breeches, 2 overall coats, 2 pairs of dungarees, 6 pairs of stockings, 3 shirts, 1 pair of ankle boots, 1 pair of shoes, 1 pair of gumboots or boots with leggings, 1 hat, 1 overcoat with shoulder titles, 1 oilskin or mackintosh, 2 towels, an oilskin sou'-wester, a green armlet, and a metal badge. After every six months of satisfactory service she receives a half-diamond to be sewn on the armlet; she has a special armlet after two years' service, and a scarlet armlet to replace the two-year one after four years' service.

Every twelve months she is entitled to some uniform replacement. All uniform is of course given free of charge, though she has to surrender a certain number of coupons.

Guaranteed Employment Week
While members of the WLA work generally under the ordinary conditions which apply to agriculture, the Land Army as a nationally organised body has found it necessary to adopt certain minimum conditions of employment as the basis on which labour will be supplied. These conditions (March, 1944) are as follows:-

Members of the Women's Land Army are supplied on the understanding that they will be employed on the basis of a guaranteed weekly wage covering a working week of not more

189

than 48 hours in winter and not more than 50 hours in summer, the weekly wage to be payable without deduction in respect of periods of bad weather or absence from work on account of sickness.

Notice – Should an employer wish to dispense with the services of a member of the Women's Land Army, one week's notice must be given from pay day, or alternatively one week's wages paid in lieu of notice.

Wages – Minimum wage and overtime rates applicable to employed members of the Women's Land Army are those laid down for women agricultural workers by the Agricultural Wages Board for the county where the worker is employed, always provided that:

(*a*) A worker of eighteen years of age or over in no case receives in respect of a working week of up to forty-eight hours in winter, or up to fifty hours in summer, a cash wage of less than 22s. 6d. after deduction has been made to cover board and lodgings provided by her employer, or after she herself has met her board and lodging charges in a billet found for her by her employer and approved by the Women's Land Army.

(*b*) A worker between the ages of seventeen and eighteen in no case receives in respect of a working week of up to forty-eight hours in winter, or up to fifty hours in summer, a cash wage of less than 18s. after deduction has been made to cover board and lodging provided by her employer, or after she herself has met her board and lodging charges in a billet found for her by her employer and approved by the Women's Land Army.

Additional payment must be made for hours worked in excess of forty-eight hours in winter or fifty hours in summer at the statutory overtime rates fixed for the county of employment under the Agricultural Wages Board's Orders.

Holidays – Members of the Women's Land Army are entitled to all holidays with pay laid down under the Orders of the Agricultural Wages Board, but no member of the Women's Land Army shall receive an annual holiday with pay of less than six working days (or seven in the case of a worker employed on the basis of a seven day working week), which holiday should normally be given as a continuous week and at a time convenient to the employer after the member of the Land Army concerned has been six months in Land Army employment.

Working hours should be planned so as to reduce Sunday work as much as possible. Every employed member of the Women's Land Army should be able to count upon a weekly half-holiday and upon an occasional long weekend. When working time is missed because a long weekend has been arranged, the time so lost may be made up by agreement with the employer, although this need not be done unless he so desires. It is to be noted that when time lost at a weekend is made up, the worker may have a claim to overtime pay in respect of some or all of the hours so worked.

Members of the Women's Land Army have the workers' usual title to the public holidays.

A free return rail warrant covering her journey home will be provided by the Women's Land Army to each volunteer who is working twenty miles or more from her home as soon after each completed six month of satisfactory service as a visit home can be arranged for her.

Sickness – If a member of the Women's Land Army is absent from work through sickness within the period of her working week, the week's wages must be paid in full without deduction and, for longer periods of absence through sickness, the weekly wage must continue to be paid in full until the employer gives one week's notice from pay day and until that notice has expired. After the expiry of the week's notice, if the employer wishes to retain a call on the worker's services when she is again fit for work, he must pay a retaining fee at least sufficient to cover the worker's cost of board and lodging or, alternatively, must himself provide her with board and lodging free of cost.

Clubs and News Letters

WLA Clubs exist in many centres both large and small. A Government grant is available for the purchase of equipment, games, wireless set, gramophone, etc.

Most counties issue a news letter free of charge, either monthly or quarterly, giving WLA information of county interest.

Appendix X
Women's Land Army Hostels

NUMBER OF HOSTELS

January, 1944.   696 Hostels.   475 run by Women's Land Army.
146 run by Young Women's
Christian Association.
75 run by War Agricultural
Executive Committees.

PERSONNEL ACCOMMODATED

22,000 Land Girls (approximately).
2,300 Staff (approximately)

TYPES OF HOSTELS

Castles, Manor Houses, Old Rectories, Hotels, Roadhouses,
Cottages, Sports Pavilions, Converted Stables, Ministry of
Works Hutments, and Converted Chicken Houses.

REQUISITIONING BODIES

Requisitioned by Women's Land Army, War Agricultural
Executive Committee or Ministry of Works, or taken over from
other Government Departments.

SIZE

Average size: 25-35 girls, but they range from 10–120.

STAFF

(a) *Pioneer Wardens* sent by Headquarters to supervise the opening of new hostels, and to cope with any crises, either domestic or disciplinary, in hostels already open.

(b) *Wardens* – entirely responsible for management of hostel and staff and for welfare of girls. In small hostels the Warden acts as a cook-housekeeper, and is therefore responsible for cooking and housework, with daily help.

(c) *Assistant Warden Cooks.*

(d) *Cooks and Assistant Cooks.*

(e) *Domestics.* (Some were recruited from Eire before the restrictions on travel were imposed.)

(f) *Daily women* (upon whom we are increasingly forced to rely).

(g) *Handymen.* (Many hostels are in very isolated positions, and handymen have to maintain electric pumps, electric light engines, as well as do odd jobs and care for the garden.)

(h) *Married couples* – we have found that married couples are successful in medium-sized hostels, particularly when they are isolated. The wife always acts as Warden and the husband as Handyman.

EQUIPMENT

This is all supplied by the Ministry of Works.

Common rooms are supplied with easy chairs and tables.

Girls sleep in dormitories in beds or double bunks (beds are supplied for all Sick Bays, for the Warden and Staff).

The girls have one kit box each, and they share one wardrobe between two, one chest of drawers between two.

Each volunteer also has a drawer which locks in which she may keep personal possessions of value.

ACCOMMODATION

There is always a dining-room and recreation-room and, where possible, a quiet room.

Care is taken to see that there is an adequate number of bathrooms, lavatories and wash-basins, and a plentiful supply of hot water to meet the demands of all residents in the hostel.

There is a laundry and drying-room in most hostels, and where electricity is available, an electric iron is supplied for the volunteers.

The Warden is always given a bedroom and sitting-room, or if this is not possible, a large bed-sitting room.

Cooks and Assistant Wardens usually have their own bed-sitting rooms and domestics share bedrooms.

In all the larger hostels a staff sitting-room is also provided.

AMENITIES

An allowance is made to each hostel out of which piano, wireless set, sewing machine, sports equipment, etc., can be bought.

The Young Women's Christian Association manage 146 hostels on behalf of the Women's Land Army, and with their wide experience of welfare work certainly do everything possible to make the volunteers healthy and happy, and at the same time give them educational and recreative facilities.

Health

On arrival at the hostel the volunteers are asked to produce their Medical Cards, and are advised to be put on the local doctor's panel as soon as possible. The Warden is naturally responsible for the health of all volunteers in the hostel, but any advice she feels she needs can be obtained from the panel doctor. He is also asked to suggest further remedies, which should be kept in stock in the hostel by the Warden as a supplementary measure to the First Aid Kit supplied by the Ministry of Works.

A careful record of sickness is kept by the Warden of each hostel, and a return sent in monthly to Headquarters. Statistics based on these returns show that the average varies between three to five per cent.

Food

Hostels are registered as Catering Establishments under Industrial Category A, and as such are entitled to special allowances of rationed and priority foods.

Wardens' Conferences

These are held from time to time in the counties, and are very popular. Headquarters Organisers, Medical Officers of Health, and representatives of the Ministry of Food are invited to speak on the different aspects of Hostel Management, and the Wardens have an opportunity of discussing their various difficulties, and also a chance to meet each other and compare notes.

Hostel Gardens

At some of the hostels the garden attached to the house is also requisitioned, and here the volunteers benefit tremendously by having fresh vegetables from the garden daily. Many of the hutment hostels have a certain amount of land attached to them which is ploughed up by the War Agricultural Executive Committees, and there is great competition among the Wardens as to who can show the prettiest and most productive garden.

Welfare

In all hostels volunteers are encouraged to form their own House Committee, which is responsible to the Warden for discipline in the hostel, and also for organising recreational activities. The following activities are encouraged:

Dances.

Whist Drives.

Make and Mend Classes.

First Aid Classes.

Lectures on all subjects such as Health, Child Welfare, Current Events.

Keep Fit Classes.

Etc.

The Warden is advised by the County Office to make the hostel the centre of the social life of the neighbourhood, and to throw it open, not only to the villagers, but also to other Land-Girls who are accommodated in private billets.

BACK TO THE LAND

WORDS BY
P. Adkins, WLA 28299 & J. Moncrieff

MUSIC BY
E. K. Loring, WLA 2053

Back to the Land, we must all lend a hand,
To the farms and the fields we must go.
There's a job to be done,
Though we can't fire a gun
We can still do our bit with the hoe.
When your muscles are strong
You will soon get along,
And you'll think that a country life's grand.
We're all needed now,
We must all speed the plough,
So come with us – Back to the Land.

Back to the Land, with its clay and its sand,
Its granite and gravel and grit,
You grow barley and wheat
And potatoes to eat
To make sure that the nation keeps fit.
Remember the rest
Are all doing their best,
To achieve the results they have planned
We will tell you once more
You can help win the war
If you come with us – Back to the Land.

Single copies 1d. each, 2d. post free, or 12 for 1s., post free, can be obtained from the Editor,
'The Land Girl', Balcombe Place, Balcombe, Hayward's Heath, Sussex
(Words and music by Land-girls)

199

PICTURE CREDITS

Page 67

Land Girl Dorothy Sills (aged 19) from Middlesborough helps with the harvest on a farm in Yorkshire. She was a shop assistant before joining the Women's Land Army. She is shown helping with the threshing, by carrying a large sack of wheat on her shoulders.

(WIKIMEDIA COMMONS D10778)

Page 69

Three Land girls harvest flax in a field which had been derelict the previous year. One woman drives the tractor as the two others sit at the rear on the flax-pulling 'trailer'.

(WIKIMEDIA COMMONS D9617)

Page 73

Two Land girls stand in the doorway of the large drag-line excavator that is being used to create ditches to improve drainage along this stretch of land. The land will then be available for arable used and to graze animals.

(WIKIMEDIA COMMONS D9783)

Page 76

Land Girl May Edwards drives a tractor past a ditcher crane on a Cambridgeshire fen. She is towing a trailer which contains other members of the Land Army and a pile of roots of the rushes and reeds which they have just removed from this newly reclaimed fen land.

(WIKIMEDIA COMMONS D8460)

Page 78

Land girls Ivy Reid, Alice Crook, Joy Godsall and a colleague dig an old bog oak out of this piece of reclaimed fen land in Cambridgeshire. The original caption stated that this tree was over 100 years old.

(WIKIMEDIA COMMONS D8463)

Page 83

A Land girl collecting cherries during World War I.

(WIKIMEDIA COMMONS Q30846)

Page 86

A welcome tea break.

(WIKIMEDIA COMMONS D11258)

Page 93

Once the lambs are born that is by no means the end of the matter.

(WIKIMEDIA COMMONS)